To the Edge of the Sea

Schooldays of a Crofter's Child

Christina Hall

Birlinn

First Published in 1999 by
Birlinn Limited
West Newington House
10 Newington Road
Edinburgh EH9 1QS

www.birlinn.co.uk

Reprinted 2002

ISBN 1 84158 021 X

British Library Cataloguing in Publication Data
A catalogue record for this book is available
from the British Library

Typeset by Textype, Cambridge
Printed and bound in Great Britain by
Creative Print and Design Wales, Ebbw Vale

For Colin

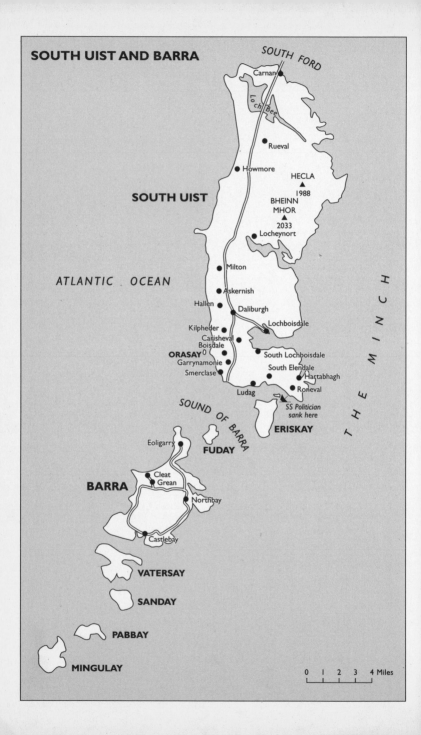

SOUTH UIST AND BARRA

SOUTH FORD

Carnan

Loch Bee

SOUTH UIST

Rueval

Howmore

HECLA
▲
1988
BHEINN
MHOR
▲
2033
Locheynort

ATLANTIC OCEAN

Milton

Askernish

Hallen
Daliburgh
Lochboisdale

Kilpheder
Canisheval
Boisdale
ORASAY
0
South Lochboisdale
Garrynamonie
South Elendale
Smerclase
Hartabhagh
Ludag
Roneval
SS Politician
sank here
ERISKAY

SOUND OF BARRA

Eoligarry
FUDAY

BARRA
Cleat
Grean
Northbay

Castlebay

VATERSAY

SANDAY

PABBAY

MINGULAY

THE MINCH

0 1 2 3 4 Miles

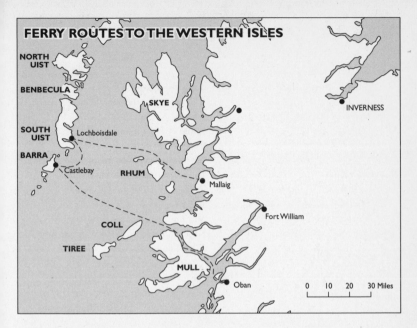

FERRY ROUTES TO THE WESTERN ISLES

NORTH UIST

BENBECULA

SOUTH UIST

BARRA

Lochboisdale

Castlebay

SKYE

RHUM

Mallaig

Fort William

COLL

TIREE

MULL

Oban

INVERNESS

0   10   20   30 Miles

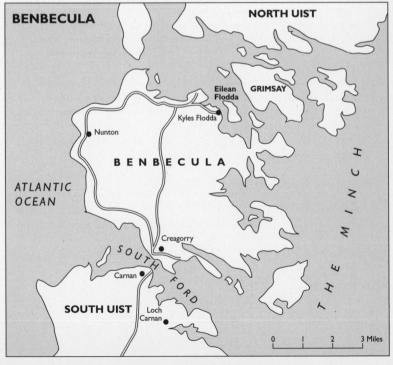

BENBECULA

NORTH UIST

Eilean Flodda

GRIMSAY

Kyles Flodda

Nunton

BENBECULA

ATLANTIC OCEAN

Creagorry

SOUTH FORD

Carnan

THE MINCH

SOUTH UIST

Loch Carnan

0   1   2   3 Miles

An óige	Youth

'Nuair dh'fhosglas sùil an òg uain
bhàin
Ri taobh a mhàthair air an raon
Seallaidh feanag air a fiaradh
Anns an iarmailt os a chionn
Tha sligh a bhradain cinnteach
cruaidh
A dìreadh suas ri eas nan gleann
Dh'ain'eoin riaslaidh, cuileag iasgair
Airson lian a chuir mo cheann
An tug thu 'n aire air aodan pàisde
'S e na thàmh an cadal trom
Saighead cràidh is crith na chom.
Cuiradh manadh na tha'n dàn dha –
Nach math nach fiosrach dhuin 'nar
'n òige
Gach lot 's gach leon, gach bròn 's
gach tàir,
Gach feanag 's iasgair tha air triall-ne
Gach lian is riasladh tha air sàil
Tha clann òg an latha 'n diugh
Mar bha clann an latha 'n dé
Cho beag de chùram ris an druid
Cho saor de dreagh ri'n dealain dé
Na bi ro throm air an fhear bheag
Ach crom ri thaobh is bì ris còir
Oir thig ealach trom an uallaich
Air a ghuailean tràth gu leòr.

The lamb newborn surveys the world
Close to its mother on the hill
Above, the crow, behind a cloud
Looks down and notes it for a kill.
The salmon's task is never easy
He toils against the stream instead
Despite his guile, the angler's fly
Will cast a net around his head.
Reflect upon an infant's face
So calm and quiet sleeping near
Some ghostly hint of what awaits him
Makes him shake and cry in fear.
What a blessing that in youth
We give no thought to future woes
The anglers and the crows that trail us
Each net, each struggle still unknown.
The children that we see today
Are like the child of yesteryear,
As free from worry as the skylark
Like butterflies they know no fear.
So don't begrudge your child his
childhood.
Bend down beside him, show him love
For life with all its heavy burdens
Will stoop his shoulders soon enough.

– translated by the author

Donald John MacMillan, 1980

Chapter One

WITH SHAKING KNEES AND gasping breath I squeezed myself as far as I could under the kitchen bench. It was a tight fit, warm, in a musty, smelly way. I tried to avoid the shoes and Wellington boots and fend off the welcoming licks of Scot, who was thumping his tail at this unusual invasion of his sleeping quarters. My two brothers were in there too, giggling, the way boys do when they are terrified and loving it. I could see it coming, leaving a fan-shaped track in the fine white sand on the stone floor. Its claw as it passed my father's size-ten boot was exactly the same length! 'It can't get over the rail.' I whispered to my brothers. 'We're safe in here.' At that moment two eyes appeared, two stalks waved over the rail, inches from my face, and I wet myself.

'For the love of God, man, stop playing with that lobster and get it in the pot before it dies of old age.'

We crept out of our hiding place and joined my father and mother admiring the latest victim of his croman, the piece of bent wire with which he tickled the lobster, teasing it, until it grabbed the croman in its huge claw and was caught. 'Aye, Kate, the Sgeir Mhór (Big Rock) has hidden him for the last time. Winston Churchill himself won't have a finer dinner today.' The massive lobster was dropped in the pot and we three children breathed again.

I was born in a crofter's thatched cottage, on the Hebridean island of South Uist, the third child in a family of six, roughly one hundred years after Gordon of Cluny's Highland Clearances and a year before the start of Adolf Hitler's World War. On an island predominantly Catholic since Saint Patrick founded the See of the Isles in the fifth century, it was a matter of pride to fill a whole pew with healthy children and family planning simply meant working out how many children you could sleep in a bed if you used the head and the foot.

How do I describe the land of my birth? The place where we say up south and down north? The island of South Uist is both beautiful and ugly. A heavenly place on a calm early morning, in Kilpheder, looking across the Gortain and Clach Ghlas towards Carisheval, when the call of the curlew and the distant sigh of the sea seem to be the only sounds left on earth. Travel south and east to the scenic village of South Lochboisdale and right at the tip you will find Rudha. There look across the bay to the busy harbour of North Lochboisdale, where, sheltered by Ben Kenneth, fishing boats, their size diminished by distance, bob at anchor. All around you the rich soil brought from Russia as ballast in empty boats and dumped in what was then the Harbourmaster's yard has produced a lush country garden at odds with the rugged terrain beyond its walls. Go north to Rueaval and drive to the summit; ignore the radar base and instead turn your eyes towards the sea. The islands of the Hebrides rise up before you and you can see the Monachs and St Kilda on a clear day. You will say, 'What a lovely island.'

Wait until a force ten gale makes your feet take you where you don't want to go and the sky looks as if the sun doesn't live there any more. When the wind abates walk out to Hartabagh, along the old hill road, and see the ruins of sad little houses once home to crofters driven to the very edge of the island by their landlord's greed. See the evidence of their struggle for survival in the crop scars on the heather-clad hillside and be grateful that the two hours of hill walking which bring you back to twentieth century Uist are all that is required of you. As you pass the lochs try not to notice the noble salmon in their man-made watery compounds, leaping in vain as their instincts tell them to swim to freedom while they wait to be starved, bled and smoked to tempt palates which can afford such delicacies. Comfort yourself by the thought that many islanders benefit financially from this sin against nature, and it is called survival, in a place where your sheep are bought for fifty pence. Beautiful and ugly, it's a place that I love more than I admit even to myself and if I could give a city child one gift, I would give him or her the gift of a summer in South Uist.

Life was basic but not too difficult by the time I was born, and we certainly never went hungry. Most families had livestock. Cattle on the land in the summer, crops with which to feed them in winter, sheep grazing on the hills, hens and ducks and sometimes a horse or two and the bounty of the sea all around us. Lobsters under rocks, herring, mackerel and many other kinds of fish to buy for pennies when the boats came in. Salmon was not for us, although the rivers bristled with them; they were the property of the Estate and the mainland anglers who could afford the permits. However that is not to say that we never ate salmon – even a gamekeeper has to sleep sometime.

Running a croft was hard work for the crofter and his wife, and as soon as the children could understand simple instructions they were expected to help. The older children looked after the little ones and allowed the mother to get on with milking and other outside chores, feeding young calves, who had been separated from their mothers, setting the milk in wide basins in the cream shed, skimming off the thick cream from other basins and storing it in crocks for churning, and the many other tasks which running a croft involve. As the children grew so their workload was increased. If you were big enough to do it you did it.

This system meant that I came close to death or at least brain damage in early infancy. I was left in a cradle under the supervision of two brothers aged four and three while my mother milked the cows. She was in a byre just behind the house and nearly jumped out of her skin when they rushed in shouting, 'He killed the girl!' 'No, it was him. He killed the girl!' The milk pail went flying and my mother ran into the house to find the cradle up-ended, with its rockers in the air. Fortunately she had used a harness to strap me in and there I was dangling upside down, about six inches above the stone floor.

Apparently, the boys had been having a rocking competition which had gone wrong. My mother was deeply shocked and asked one of the neighbours how she coped with her brood of toddlers and the outside work. 'I have no trouble' said the woman 'I get a piece of rope and tie them all to the bench'. Today's social services would not approve. However, the family in question grew up tall and strong and pillars of the community with no need for counselling.

4

The island, even then, was no longer an island on its own, as it had been in the early thirties when my mother was nearly drowned crossing the South Ford, which separated South Uist from its nearest neighbour, the then island of Benbecula. Fed by the Atlantic on one side and the Minch on the other, currents and tides in that sandy stretch were treacherous, and the crossing at low tide was achieved by means of what in those days was called a 'machine'. This was special horse-drawn carriage used for carrying people and post across from one island to another. The coachman had a mature and experienced horse between one pair of shafts and was breaking in a young horse on the other side. It was a dark evening with a rising wind and he was anxious to complete the journey quickly, as it was dangerously close to the time when one of the channels he had to cross would fill with rushing water and become a death trap. The horses were good swimmers and in normal circumstances the high wheels of the machine would still have sufficient purchase on the sand to ensure a safe crossing.

Whether the young horse sensed the imminent danger or not we shall never know, but from the start of the journey it was difficult to control, and with the wind rising and the tide coming in it was a frightening situation. The coachman saw that it was too late to turn back. Behind him the tide had turned, so on he went. As the water got deeper the old horse showed no fear and simply launched itself smoothly into a swimming motion. The young horse, however, went completely crazy and tried to climb into the machine. The passengers faced certain death as the water got deeper and the rising wind carried their cries for help out to the Atlantic. On the Benbecula side one of the MacAulays from Creagorry Hotel was tying up a gate which had broken loose in the high wind and he heard what he thought was a play on the wireless coming from inside the hotel. When he went in and saw that the guests were eating and just talking quietly to each other he realised that the faint sounds of mortal fear came from the South Ford. He quickly organised a rescue party, just in time. The coachman and passengers were lucky: they survived, but the young horse drowned. In his panic he caught his hind legs in the harness and the tide did the rest. The other horse was cut loose and swam to safety. From that day my mother had the greatest fear of water going over her head and when she washed her hair we could hear her making little whimpering noises.

In 1942 a causeway was built linking the two islands and twenty-seven years later the completion of the North Ford Causeway joined the island of North Uist to its neighbours. As the Outer Hebrides had been erroneously called 'The Long Island', since the days when the receding Ice Age left the inlets between them still frozen, now at least the Uists and Benbecula fitted that description.

Money, in my young days, came from the sale of cattle and a few Government subsidies. Of course there was also a workforce in paid employment including the ones who supplemented their income by gathering seaweed as their ancestors had done. My father and his peers sold it on at a fair rate, to a factory where it was burnt and the fine alkaline ash was then shipped out to manufacturers of such diverse goods as soap, glass, table jelly and orangeade. Their ancestors, MacDonald of ClanRanald's crofters, cut it for nothing as part payment for the lease of their bit of land. They also burned it in bothies and had to collect twenty to thirty tons of kelp to produce one ton of ash. This was sold by ClanRanald for around twenty pounds per ton. My father told me about this and said that much of the ash went to France and that the Napoleonic Wars put an end to the trade; so in his day it was only done on a much smaller scale.

The island was a place where you worked hard and brought your family up to do likewise. We all want our children to have a better life than we had and in this respect my parents were no different to any town dweller; they wanted us all to have the chances which they themselves had missed.

For my parent's generation, education had been a hit-or-miss affair. All the schools were run by English-speaking masters who did not even acknowledge the existence of the Gaelic language, despite introducing the brighter children to Latin and Greek. One of our neighbours once saw my brother doing his Latin homework and said, 'I know all about 'Mensa . . . mensae . . . feminine . . . a table'. This man could not read or write a word of Gaelic but knew the Latin declension for table. The children were taught in a tongue which they did not understand, for much of the time. Pupil teachers and a few Gaelic-speaking assistants had the task of teaching little island children a foreign language so that they could understand their lessons. With such a system, coupled with frequent absences when the children had to help with the croft work, only the brightest and most ambitious pupils stood a chance. Despite this situation many fine scholars emerged to make their mark in various fields. Far from being the idle, witless, drunken lot so described by A.A. MacGregor in his book *The Western Isles*, the islanders have always been tough, resourceful and intelligent. Without their quick wits they would not have survived exploitation through many generations. It's a pity that certain authors did not take the time or trouble to get to know this before rushing into print.

Although they worked hard at it, neither my mother nor my father were natural crofters. She was a good-looking young woman who had left the island to work on the mainland, first as a lady's-maid to a Lady Patten-McDougal in Oban, and then on to Oban Cottage Hospital where she got bitten by the nursing bug and went on to Hawkhead Asylum in Glasgow to work with the mentally ill. She loved life away from the island and was in the throes of a romance with a young doctor when the summons came to come back home and look after her mother, who had broken her hip. My mother was reluctant to return but things were desperate at home and her sister Catherine, a teacher, bought her a piano as a sort of consolation gift. She was very musical and used to sing at mòds (Gaelic Festivals) and ceilidhs and that helped her to cope with her changed life. The romance with the doctor did not survive the parting and some years later she met a young man called Tormad Ruadh (Red-haired Norman) MacMillan, when they were both singing at a ceilidh in his native Benbecula and subsequently married him.

As a younger son in a family of boys, my father probably had little knowledge of croft work when he married her. (By tradition the older boys would shoulder most of the work in the knowledge that they were going to inherit their father's land and the land of unmarried or childless uncles.) Tenure of the crofts was handed down from father to son. If the son happened to have ten sisters older than him then that was their hard luck. When there were no sons then the land usually went to the first son-in-law in the line of succession.

My maternal grandfather had lost his eldest son in a tragic case of medical misdiagnosis. He was being treated for a stomach ulcer and his appendix, which was the real problem, burst. That same year had seen the worst epidemic of flu that the island had ever known. It hit my grandparents hard as they lost one of their daughters and the baby of the family, a little boy. My grandmother was so ill that her children were dead and buried before she could be told about her loss. The death of the last male heir meant that when my grandfather died, my father, the only son-in-law and an incomer from Benbecula, became a South Uist crofter.

From an early age we children were urged to study hard and get qualifications which would open doors to a better life. By then education on the island had much improved and even now, after a lifetime of teaching all over the world, I think that Uist schools were up there with the best.

The idea of 'getting on' and 'doing well' meant passing exams and leaving the island to go to senior school and then on to university. So, sadly, many gifted islanders left, never to return. In my own family, all six of us joined the exodus, leaving my parents with an empty nest for many years. They had always encouraged us to do well and get on and in so doing lost us to the outside world. Fortunately the call of the island is strong and one returned to live on the croft, while the rest of us maintained the link and have spent much time on the island over the years.

The first step towards achieving this exile was taken for me at the age of four and a half. My mother and father literally gave me away. They figured that my chances of getting on would be much enhanced if my two maiden aunts (my mother's sisters) brought me up, away from the rough and tumble of croft life in a very small cottage with an ever-increasing population. I was not given a choice. It was presented to me as a privilege and I was told to be very well-behaved so as to be deserving of such good fortune, and I felt very important.

One aunt, Catherine, was headmistress of a school in Benbecula, and the other, Christina, acted as her housekeeper. In their youth they may have been lovers of the bright lights, like my mother, but if so by the time I joined them the impulses had long gone. They were good women in the full sense of the word. They lived blameless lives and spent a lot of it on their knees saying the rosary. All my educational and material needs were well met. They worried about me and often told me that they must be mad to take on 'someone else's property'; my place in Heaven was constantly sought but it was a lonely time.

The schoolhouse where my aunts lived in Kyles Flodda was a large house with very high ceilings, and after the cosy croft house it was a bit frightening. There was a big spare room which housed all sorts of junk left there by the previous occupant and I used to play among the boxes. I remember finding a big fox fur with glass eyes, and that was my dog, Scot. I hugged it and talked to it until one day its head fell off and I gave it a lovely funeral, playing the part of priest, choir and congregation till Auntie Chirsty caught me and told me to stop being blasphemous or the devil would come and get me. School was the only life I knew, so I played 'schools'. The teacher aunt told me stories of her days at college and read messages that her student friends had written in a little red book. I could picture scenes of great companionship. Happy girls being taught to be teachers by kindly nuns. So a new game evolved: 'Packing my bag for the Convent.'

The highlight of the week was a trip to the shop. By now the war was well underway and many items were no longer available. On the way to the shop my aunt would tell me about fruit and sweets which were nothing more than a fond memory for her and a complete mystery to me. She described a banana. "It is a long yellow thing and you open it by pulling a strip down on one side."

'Ah,' I thought. 'it has a zip.'

'The inside is sweet and creamy,' said she.

'Filled with cake,' thought I.

Big disappointment in the banana department is my abiding memory of peace being declared.

The shop was on Island Flodda, which was a tidal island. Now it too has a little causeway, but then we had to be careful not to take too long over the shopping or we would have to stay overnight with the owners. This happened one night and I really enjoyed staying with the kindly Currie family. After a lovely meal of fried *sgadan ùr* (fresh herring) they settled down to share the local news with auntie and didn't mind if I asked questions, as children do. There was much excitement as a young man from Roshinish was well on the way to being ordained as a priest and if he actually finished the course, he would be the first priest to come from Benbecula in living memory. They all knew why this would be such an auspicious occasion, but I didn't, so they told me about the 'Curse of Nunton'.

Nunton, situated at the south end of Culla Bay, between Aird and Griminish, used to be the traditional seat of MacDonald of Clanranald. Gaelic folklore has it that many centuries ago a Convent stood there, hence the name Nun-town. Ripples of anti-Papist feeling, following the Reformation, spread as far as the islands, and the convent was destroyed. The nuns suffered deaths too awful to contemplate: some were burned, some buried alive, and the Abbess and her main helpers were staked out at the waters edge to drown by degrees under the incoming tide. With her dying breath the Abbess cursed the island and decreed that no priest would ever come from Benbecula.

According to the Curries the story was true: the nuns had existed; folklore said so. The curse had been effective until that time and now it looked as if it was about to be lifted. It would be nice if I could say that they got their wish. However, some time later, shortly before his ordination, the young man from Roshinish suffered a nervous breakdown and left the seminary. Who knows if the stories about the nuns are fact or fiction, but there was one very nervous child sleeping in a strange bed on Island Flodda that night.

On the way home auntie sat down and rested once we crossed the ford, and I played in the rock pools where 'partain' (little crabs) scurried. I thought about being staked out waiting for the tide to engulf me and decided that I would probably have been too frightened to curse anybody.

My parents came to visit now and then, and once they left my brothers with us for a week. It was a time like no other for me. I'm sure my poor aunts never forgot it either. The boys were high-spirited and as just about everything was forbidden, they spent all their time there finding ways to outwit the minders. We sneaked out and played on the shore and the boys came back with pockets full of 'partain'. That night when we were all kneeling down in our nightwear saying the rosary, in the middle of the third Sorrowful mystery the crabs were released. They headed, as if programmed, towards the aunties' bare feet. I went into fits of hysterical laughter and the

12

aunties leapt around, screeching, while the boys tried to capture the invaders. We had to re-start the rosary several times and each time one of us laughed, auntie intoned, 'The first Sorrowful mystery, The Agony in the Garden,' again. We had sore knees in the morning and the boys were sent home.

War brought many changes to island life. A military base was established in Balivanich and the school there was requisitioned for use by the personnel. We children hoped that they would ask for our school too, but no luck. There was talk of huge planes called Flying Fortresses frightening the cows, but the tales of enemy U-boats being sunk by the brave young fliers and the awful losses of so many of their own numbers swung island opinion in their favour. Besides which the NAAFI and other establishments in Balivanich provided employment and excitement for the locals. The 'airmen', as they were known, embraced island life and I believe, although this is only hearsay, that many of the local girls embraced the airmen. Well, there was a war on, so who could blame them. Not I. Many years later I met, married and have had a great life with a handsome young soldier who was serving on the self-same base.

A bartering system between the service personnel and the locals meant that many goods in short supply were exchanged for eggs, chickens, butter, potatoes, cream etc., and that's how I first tasted chocolate. The aunties had contacts and managed to get a packet of Swiss chocolates. I was given one after dinner every night and to this day they are my favourite sweet.

It was the age of expedience, and, as the camp had a well-equipped hospital, the local doctor organised a mass tonsilectomy for all children who had tonsils. Well, that's what it looked like as I lay in a Nissen hut with what seemed like the entire child population of the planet. The noise was horrendous as they all cried for their mammies. I could hardly remember my mammy and I certainly wasn't going to cry for the aunties, but it seemed the right thing to do. So I cried too.

A voice from the next bed said, 'Hey you! Come and see what I've found.' I stopped crying and followed this older girl into the bathroom at the end of the hut. Neither of us had seen a bathroom with porcelain fittings before but we just knew that all was not as it should be. There, in the washbasin, was a large turd. Obviously some parent had not told their child which appliance was which. There was a very stern lecture on disgusting behaviour that night. That incident and being given ice-cream for my sore throat are my only memories of the airmen.

School holidays meant a return to the family. At Gramsdale I was put on *Bus a Mhullaich* (The Mull man's bus), a rickety conveyance, with much wood in the bodywork, which creaked its way from one end of the island to the other, delivering goods and people, very slowly, to various destinations. The journey was long and the talk among the adult passengers was mostly about the war. Much merriment was caused by the news that some crofts close to Balivanich airfield now had red lights on their roofs. The driver's insistence that it was a safety precaution for landing aircraft only gave rise to more ribald speculation, and there was shock at the news that a Benbecula girl had 'gone and married one'. The old men talked longingly of the exciting lives the young airmen led and how brave they were to fly a plane even without 'Jerry' trying to shoot them out of the sky. This sobering thought usually turned the conversation to the news from their own young men who were in various branches of the services, and I lost interest as I counted off the landmarks between me and home. Creagorry, where there were parcels and sacks of mail for the hotel. The 'New Bridge' over the South Ford, unexciting if the tide was in, but spanning sands full of cockle-pickers if it was out. Carnan, where the driver got out for a cup of tea. Then across Loch Bee, where the waters were flung over the bus if the day was stormy and anglers stood waist high in the loch if the day was fine. Beinn na Coraraidh, where the road took a hairpin bend and plunged downwards with much shrieking from the passengers. Then Askernish and Daliburgh where I started to look for the smoke from our chimney, till we stopped at Kilpheder cross roads and my brothers got up from the verge where they had been sitting against the post-box waiting for the bus to arrive. As we walked the half mile or so home we caught up on our respective lives. Their stories were always so much more interesting than mine, and at the age of six they taught me to smoke.

Chapter Two

MANY OF THE YOUNG men from the villages were on active service, and sadly many were lost. My father, after a short time with the Lovat Scouts, was given an exemption. The Department of Agriculture provided him with a tractor so that he could help other families who were short of labour on their crofts. He was also a member of the Home Guard. Like the series 'Dad's Army' they were often out on exercise and our little windows in the croft house were faithfully blacked out every night; but thankfully they didn't actually make contact with the enemy. Once or twice his paratrooper brothers called in to see us, when on leave, looking very handsome in their uniforms, but very tired and strained, and he would look sad for a long time after they left. I don't know whether he wished that he was going with them, but I think he was anxious for their safety.

The spirit of community was high and peat-cutting and harvesting of crops were all done on a basis of 'We'll do yours today and you'll come and help with mine tomorrow.' Thus everybody managed to complete their tasks without feeling beholden to anyone. Island sense of pride and dignity prevailed.

Peat-cutting day was very festive. Sometimes my father would do a bit of cutting by himself, but the bulk of the hard, black peat which was burned in the shiny black Enchantress stove which kept us warm, boiled water and provided heat for cooking, was cut by a team of friends operating on the terms which I have just mentioned. They would have breakfast and their evening meal at our house but at mid-day we took food out to them. One or more of the men's wives would come to help my mother prepare a substantial pile of sandwiches, hard-boiled eggs and freshly made scones and pancakes, spread with crowdie and cream over butter from our own churn. This was loaded into the wicker washing basket and we all set off over the heather to the workers. I can still recall the squishing of water between my toes and the prickling of heather on the soles of my bare feet as we played our way out to the bogs.

We could hear the men talking, singing and laughing long before we got there and this added to the sense of occasion. They'd stop their work and build a fire on the bank to brew tea in a three-legged pot, before sitting round the crisp white sheet which we had spread on the ground and covered with food. Peaty hands were merely wiped on the grass and the food was consumed. Extravagant compliments were paid to my mother for producing such regal fare, and many amusing anecdotes would be exchanged about the morning's work. We children admired the large slabs of peat and found new games to play, well away from the deep watery trench of the bog. After they finished eating, the 'table' was cleared and everything wrapped in the cloth and put back in the basket. The menfolk smoked a cigarette or a pipe and got back to their work, and the children got rides home in the basket.

Once the black slabs of peat had dried on one side we children were called into service. Each slab had to be carefully turned, so that the other side could harden. Then came the gathering into table-like piles of three, with two slabs leaning towards each other and one placed on top, to let the wind blow through and complete the drying process. This was known as *togail na mònadh* (Lifting the peat), then came *cruinneachadh* (gathering) into small cone-shaped piles, still out on the bog, ready for the great day when it was brought home and stacked. You had to choose the right kind of weather for making your peat stack. If any rain got into the centre of your stack it could soon spread throughout the whole structure and make the peat damp and difficult to light. You chose large slabs of peat for the base and tried to grade it according to size as the stack grew. Building a peat stack was an art in itself, and the better the brick-like construction of the outside, the better your peat would be protected from the elements and the brighter your fire would burn through the dark Hebridean winter.

Each crofter had a piece of land on the machair, sandy fertile soil where they grew grain crops and Kerr's Pink potatoes to die for. Nowadays when I find some really outstanding potatoes I think of the machair crop. The sandy soil of the machair was fertilised by the seaweed, which lay along the shoreline in plentiful abundance. This was a messy, smelly job but all it cost the crofter was his labour. At one time the powers-that-be came up with the idea of paying the islanders a subsidy for using guano and other fertilisers instead of the traditional seaweed, and this seemed to give good results, until the machair started to blow away in the wind. The kelp had bound the sandy soil particles together in a way that man's invention simply did not. A subsidy was then paid to the crofters to collect seaweed and spread it on their land. So they ended up being paid for a task which, for centuries, they had performed for nothing.

The corn and rye were cut by hand with a scythe, a task for men only. The children helped to tie the sheaves and prop them up into stooks which were gathered together to form small stacks. Then the stacks were brought home, either by horse and cart or by tractor and made into *cruachan* (big stacks) in the stackyard. Many years into the future, my own little boys and their father helped with the machair harvest whilst home on holiday, and I heard them telling their friends what a great time they'd had. A lobster boat had come in while they were playing in the dunes and they had been given a sack of crab claws to roast over an open fire which my husband lit for them and then they rode home on the tractor. They're men now and their grandfather and the lobster fisherman are long gone; but that day still lives in their memories.

Hay in the fields round the croft was given similar treatment to the corn, only it was a much more delicate operation and the weather played a vital role. After it was cut into long swathes and the rough shaws taken out you prayed for fine weather. If it rained before it was dried, turned, dried, shaken, and dried again it would rot in the stack. It was a busy time and for me a golden time. I was back with my family and my father made me a small fork so that I could shake hay with the rest of them.

The hay was also destined for the stackyard, where it was made into a large loaf-shaped thing called a 'Dash'. While this was being built, we were hoisted up into the stack to stamp the hay down so that the finished product was compact enough to prevent pockets of gas being generated. This could make the hay hot and unsuitable for feed. Cows could be very ill if they ate it. This was my father's explanation for the procedure. I have no idea whether it is true or not, but the stamping was fun.

When the stackyard was full there was a great feeling of security, much the same as I still get now before visitors are due and I know that all their meals are planned and the shopping done. No matter what the coming winter could throw at us the cows, sheep and horses would eat and therefore so would the family. We children treated the giant stacks as an adventure playground. Great games were invented and as long as we did no climbing or in any way interfered with the lofty structures we could play our own version of 'pirates' and 'hide-and-seek' to our hearts' content.

Another annual event was the blanket wash. The canal, a wide channel of water which ran from Strome to Kilpheder machair and was regularly cleaned, provided the softest water you could wish for, and this was the venue. Usually two or three wives got together, and with their children carried a zinc bath containing the family's supply of soft white Highland blankets down to the canal. A fire was made and canal water heated in the bath. Soap flakes were added to the water as it reached the required temperature and the bath was removed from the fire. Then one by one the blankets were put in the bath and relays of willing children lifted in to dance the dirt out. The process was repeated with clean soapy water and then three rinses of warm clear water.

The women spent most of the time talking and filling and emptying and wringing and folding but we just danced all day. The clean, fluffy blankets were then spread out on the rocks to dry and once again we prayed for good weather. It is so much easier to wash your duvet cover in you washer/drier but communal blanket washing by the canal was such a grand social occasion.

Speaking of social occasions, have you ever heard of the Polly? If you've seen the film *Whisky Galore*, or read the book you can be forgiven for thinking that the people of Uist had little to do with the contents of the *Politician*. Well, think again. A whole lot of whisky and other goods found its way to Uist and Eriskay. Unfortunately the Customs man lived in Lochboisdale, so the South Uist people had a great deal of his attention. The writer, Sir Compton Mckenzie, lived on Barra at the time and wrote a novel about a wrecked ship called *The Cabinet Minister*, which was the subject of the film, shot on the beautiful island of Barra. There were some who would say that it was a bit unfair; the Barra people were not troubled by the attention of the Customs man, as he had his hands full in Uist and they also got the film.

The 'Polly', for the uninitiated, was the good ship SS *Politician* which sailed out of Mersey harbour on February 3rd, 1941 bound for Jamaica and the USA. Her cargo ranged from whisky to bicycles. There was also a large amount of Jamaican money on board, but it was of little value to the islanders by comparison with the 264,000 bottles of the finest whisky, distilled in the country which gave whisky to the world. Instead of sailing round Barra Head 'The Polly' ran aground in the Sound of Eriskay, far west of her plotted course. Many theories exist as to why this happened, and the one which makes most sense to me is that the whisky knew where it would be most appreciated.

The money: what was it for and where did it go? A

question which has been asked many times. Naturally, the purpose of shipping vast amounts of money out of the country at such a time generated many rumours on the island. Some even said that King George was feathering his nest abroad in case we lost the war. Much of it was recovered legitimately and returned to the Treasury, and as for the islanders, they were much more interested in the cases of whisky, and any notes they found were given to their children who used them to play 'shops'. Rumour, of course tells a different story, and sudden unexplained affluence in an island family's life-style can still provoke whispers of 'Polly money'.

My father and his friends sailed out to the the wreck many times, favouring the darkest nights, as the Customs and Excise man on the island was anxious that the ship with all its cargo would remain intact until it could be salvaged. When this proved impossible they towed it to Lochboisdale and blew it up. A wicked waste. Well that's how the islanders saw it as they congratulated themselves on having rescued as much of the cargo as possible. The 'rescuers' came from near and far in their little boats, and working side by side on the oily decks of a heaving ship lit only by Tilley lamps and candles, they 'liberated' as much of the cargo as their little boats could carry. Sometimes they got a bit too ambitious and piled the boat so high that they had to throw some of their spoils overboard to make room for the crew. But, as my father said, 'We knew that there was plenty more there for the taking.' Plenty there was; his average night's share was 120 bottles of whisky, the odd bolt of fine cloth, shirts, and enough bicycle parts to service the 'Tour de France'. When the Customs men stopped their searching and it was safe, he managed to make at least two good bikes out of the bits.

The raids were fraught with danger, as the most precious cargo was submerged in a hold full of oily sea water and had to be speared from above. As the wreck heaved around with the swell and the deck was covered in oil, one slip could be one too many, so one night my father thought that his time had come when he overbalanced and fell into the the hold. He was up to his shoulders in water and his legs were firmly jammed inside a bolt of cloth, too far down in the sloping hold for the men on deck to reach him with spears or rope. The boats only carried the minimum of equipment, as space was precious and the rope only had to be long enough for looping around a speared case and hoisting it on to the deck. As he struggled to save himself my father heard someone say, 'Chaill sinn Tormad bochd' ('We've lost poor Norman'), and the nearest I can come to translating his response is: 'Not bloody likely!' Somehow he found finger-holds, and using the strength of his shoulders, clawed his way to safety with the unfurling cloth still wrapped around his legs. When he made it to the deck, the entire raiding party were on their knees praying, the Protestants reciting a psalm and the Catholics chanting the prayer for the dying, 'Dia 'nochd athair nam bochd' . . . ('Lord, father of the poor, be here tonight . . .'). 'When they saw me appear,' he told us, 'they got off their knees and got on with their thieving.' It's a wonder that none of the islanders came to grief on their expeditions, because, apart from anything else, no more than a handful of them could swim.

As the years have gone by, interest in the 'Polly' has dimmed, but it takes little to rekindle it and I'm sure that the latest book, Roger Hutchinson's Polly (1990), won't be the last one we'll see. Throughout his life, my father regaled Francis Collinson of the School of Scottish

Studies and Fred McAulay of the BBC and many other broadcasters and authors with anecdotes of the period. To this day one room in the family bungalow, in Kilpheder, is called No.5. That was the hold full of oily water in which the whisky was found buried beneath a jumble of assorted cargo – in other words, a mess.

I was a very small child when it all happened but was aware that something rather special was going on. One minute it was all sighs and people talking in hushed tones about the war. We had one of the few radios in the village and always had people in, 'listening to the wireless'. We children had to be very quiet, except when the traitorous William Joyce, the Irish-American hanged for treason in 1946, whom we knew as 'Lord Haw Haw', spoke in praise of Fascism and called for British surrender; then we were encouraged to see who could produce a good fart.

Suddenly the visitors were all happy and full of suppressed excitement. My father was always getting ready to go somewhere secret at night. If any English-speaking stranger came to the door we were coached to say, in English, 'My father is out on the hill herding sheep and my mother is not in.' Fortunately our skills as decoys were never put to the test, as we often got it wrong in rehearsal and said 'My father is on the hill looking for ships.' Our closest shave came one day when I was playing outside and I saw the Customs man approaching on his bike. I called out the usual warning and my mother snatched me indoors saying, 'For the love of God, girl, your pinny is made from Polly cloth.'

Whisky was always around at that time and my younger brother was delivered by a midwife so drunk that my father had to cut the cord. Funnily enough I can't remember anyone getting nasty or any brawls resulting from the sudden deluge of 'The Water of Life', the literal translation of *Uisge Beatha*, the Gaelic for whisky, although I can recall a group of sane but sozzled men digging for the Stone of Destiny in Clach Ghlas, the field opposite our house. All know is that in the midst of the gloom of war, the entire population of a bleak and remote island always seemed to be excited and happy. But as I said, I was very young.

We made our own entertainment and didn't feel the days passing. One of the many bicycle wheels to bowl along with a stick kept me happy for hours I'm told. One day my little brother got into terrible trouble for sitting on a flat rock and smashing something to bits with a stone. At the time I couldn't see what the trouble was about but I have since discovered that the something was my mother's gold watch. He literally wanted to find the tick. As it happens, his life-long hobby has been tinkering with watches.

Little brother was named Donald, the third boy in the family to bear that name, a phenomenon not uncommon among island families. In those days you always named your children after your parents and other members of the family. Mother and father took it in turns to name the children, and as my mother's father was Angus and her brother Donald, she named her first son Donald Angus. My father's father was Donald John, so he named the second son Donald John. I was named Christina Ann, after my mother's mother and Saint Ann. I think they felt that I needed someone with an established track record to guide me through life. Then the next son was Donald after my father's brother. Later, when the twins arrived, my mother named them Mary Flora after her sister and Alick Iain after her brother. She was given the chance to choose both names as she wanted to honour her sister and brother who had died, aged eighteen and two, in the year of the flu epidemic. As Donald was a popular family name on the island from the days of the Clans you often found a family with a Donald Mór (Big Donald) and a Donald Beag (Little Donald), a Donald Joseph and a Donald Patrick and so on. The second names were always used, so it was not as confusing as it seems.

Donald was the fourth child, and as I was born between him and the two older boys they considered him a baby. When the twins joined us they were a self-contained unit from the day they could toddle, talking and playing as one and always watching each other's backs, so young Donald ploughed his own furrow and consequently became a very independent individual. He was always plinking out odd little rhythms on the piano instead of following a recognisable tune, but we were not to know that he was actually composing. Many years and many good tunes later, when his older brother, the late Donald John, wrote the popular Gaelic song 'Tioram air Tìr', it was young Donald who composed the swinging tune which made it a hit. His name did not appear on any credits or record labels due to an unintentional oversight, so now they know, little brother. His favourite playmates were the dog or the current pet lamb (one who had been rejected by its mother and had to be bottle fed). In our society the animals were there for a purpose and one day at the dinner table he asked, 'Where's Tommy, I've been looking for him all day?' My father replied, 'You're eating him.' Donald is over fifty years of age now and since that day has never eaten lamb.

Home, in my childhood, always meant the periods of time which I spent on the croft, and going back to the aunties at the start of each new term was only made bearable by the thought that there was a school holiday

26

to spend with my family at the end of it. The aunties questioned me avidly about the holiday activities and I tried to satisfy their curiosity, whilst instinctively watching my tongue, in case I told them anything which might show my parents to be less than perfect. Although I got to know Benbecula very well later on in life, my time there with the aunties produced a six-year-old who loved to read the works of Robert Louis Stevenson, but I might as well have lived on the moon for all I can remember of the the place and its people. I wasn't miserable – just waiting for the time when I could go home. When a transfer to Barra came through for the teacher auntie I thought that was it. I'd done my time. I'd been good, well, good enough, so I'd be going home now, forever.

Chapter Three

HELLO BARRA! ONCE AGAIN I said a tearful farewell to the croft and its occupants and sailed across the sea with the aunties to their new home. I stayed there until my primary education was completed and I came home at last at the age of ten and a half. The island of Barra is the southernmost of the large islands of the Outer Hebrides. If you see the string of islands as a clawless lobster, as I do, then Barra forms the tail. In the early 1900s it was the herring 'cash and carry' of the West Coast of Scotland and Castlebay was a thriving port. There the fishing vessels brought their catch and sold it to the curers, and girls from all over the Hebrides found work on the gutting, salting and packing crews. By the time I first saw Barra, the herring industry was only a memory, but there was a sense of bustle and optimism about the island that even a child could not miss. The people seemed warm and full of good humour. They are renowned for their excellent singing voices and I have memories of many a good ceilidh in the church halls.

The schoolhouse, on the borders of Grean and Cleat, was not as isolated as the one at Kyles Flodda. By the door grew a bush which was almost a tree with the sweetest-smelling white flowers. We have one in our garden now and every time I pass it, especially in the evening when the flowers are at their most fragrant, I'm back in Barra. One day I might find out what it is called. Coming from a virtually treeless island I was fascinated by it.

I was also captivated by the island itself. To me, just having read *Coral Island* this was a real island-shaped island and it seemed so much lighter and more colourful than Uist. The grass appeared to be a brighter green, the sky a lighter blue and the hills, dotted with sheep, looked smaller and more friendly than the stark majesty of Ben Mór, with its browns and greys and rocky outcrops.

Perhaps the impression was heightened by the fact that, along with most of the island children, my face had been furnished with my first pair of glasses. I really needed them, unlike most of the children who got them, threw them away and have lived their lives with perfect vision. I don't know if it was a feature of the time, or whether it was an island thing, but it seemed that you had syrup of figs and worm syrup on a Friday, tonsils out when you started school, closely followed by the arrival of glasses, and you got false teeth at the first sign of toothache, it didn't seem to have too much to do with your actual physical condition. At least I managed to hang on to my teeth.

Although Barra covers a large area, the centre of the island is rugged and mountainous, so most of the island's core is unpopulated. All the main villages are coastal and the *taobh an iar* (west coast), the subject of many songs and poems, is a serene landscape of bays and sand dunes.

Unlike Uist, where the main road system comes straight down the middle of the island, Barra is encircled by its thirteen or so miles of road. With or without spectacles it is a lovely island, and much though I love Uist, it has a harshness to the landscape which is probably due to the fact that it is long and narrow and has so much water and volcanic rock in its formation.

House-keeping auntie and I went shopping to Alasdale and we found distant cousins living there, whom we visited now and then. Their daughter was at our school and the same age as me. She was much taller than I was and fair-haired and very pretty. As if this wasn't enough, she had a kilt. At this stage in my life I discovered envy. Despite all this we became good friends – only during school hours of course. The landscape may have changed, but the aunties hadn't. They took me to church at Craigstone, and if my memory serves me right there were more relatives there, so more cups of tea after church. Then there was the biggest treat of all: a trip on the bus which went round the island, when auntie had to go to the bank at Castlebay.

Castlebay was unlike any place I had seen before. There was a real castle out in the bay, Kissimul Castle, the seat of the MacNeils of Barra, and it looked as if it had seen better days. Over the years I have learned that the island and the castle had been lost to the clan for some time and that when Robert MacNeil bought it back in 1937 it had been in very poor condition indeed. Not only was the structure itself crumbling, but bits of the castle had mysteriously disappeared and the original gate was found under a peat stack in Sponish on the island of North Uist. Robert, however, was an architect and a very determined man, and he lived to see his castle restored and lived in. It is now a place of interest and attracts visitors from all over the world, especially members of the clan. Its condition did not trouble me too much; I had never seen a castle before and in my eyes it was Camelot.

The beautiful church, Our Lady Star of the Sea, was up on the hill overlooking the commercial centre of Castlebay with its few shops and pier offices on the road named, 'The Street'. I was impressed. We used to walk past a large, stone-built, house, perched above the others, on a flower-filled, rocky site. It was called Craigard Guesthouse. I vowed that, one day, I would live in a house with that name, without the Guesthouse bit. Well, having had many homes in many countries this one is called Dùnàrd (High Mound). 'Craig' is derived from the Gaelic name for rock and we don't have one in sight, but we are on top of a hill, so it was the closest I could get. After more than fifty years I'm nearly there. The bus wound its way round the other side of the island on the way home, past Northbay, which we also visited from time to time. The people on the bus laughed and chatted and the Barra accent, slightly different to the Uist way of talking, was much in evidence. It was a cheerful, sociable kind of bus. This was the bus which I caught, on the day that I ran away.

One of our relatives in Benbecula was getting married. He had seen me once or twice when he visited the aunties at Kyles Flodda and when their wedding invitation arrived in the post there was a separate card made out just for me. Although the regime in the aunties' household was as strict as ever, I was beginning to develop a mind of my own and occasionally stood up to them.

The strap (the teacher auntie's tawse), was always brought in after school to keep me in line. Don't get me wrong, I wasn't a battered child or anything like that and I have no hang-ups whatever about the quite considerable amount of corporal punishment I received during my school life. No doubt I deserved all of it and more. All I have to say on the subject is that it was great fun earning it! They say that the abused becomes the abuser. Well, neither during my long teaching career nor while bringing up three children have I gone down that particular road.

The aunties, as I have said, were good women, but I was not their natural child. They were fond of me, and I was a headstrong brat. They proved their devotion to our family in many ways over the years, but never demonstrated any affection openly. To say that they were prudish would be an understatement. Kissing or cuddling or anything of that ilk was just foreign to their nature. It was a cold environment.

I really wanted to go to that wedding. It would mean a chance to see the family again and I had never been to a wedding and I had my own special, personal invitation. I really, really wanted to go. The aunties, however, had other ideas. It was winter and the crossing between Castlebay and Lochboisdale would be rough. Anyway, the school term was in full swing and only one auntie was free to go. This was not strictly true, as there were a number of perfectly capable relief teachers who could have stepped in for the couple of days. However they had decided and that was that. With hindsight I can see that their reasons were perfectly valid, but as I've already said, I was a headstrong brat. I waited until they were both outside doing something, then used the tin opener on my money box, put my best dress into a bag, took my invitation and hot-footed it down the hill to catch the bus to Castlebay.

Once I got there it was simple. I got on the *Loch Earn*, bought my ticket and waited for the boat to chug its way to Lochboisdale. I threw up several times, standing at the rail, clutching my bag in one hand and one of the horizontal bars in the other. I was only nine years old and pretty short for my age, so I had to stand on tip-toe when it was time to 'Call Hughie'. The boat was very busy with several children on board and nobody seemed to notice that I was travelling alone.

Inexperienced traveller though I was, I knew that a journey on the *Loch Earn* was, for me at least, the worst possible means of getting from A to B in the history of travel. I got to know the dreadful tub even better as I grew older and frequently used it to get to school on the mainland, so I know that my initial diagnosis was spot on.

I wandered about a bit, as it was very cold at the rails and people kept being sick on my shoes. One room I went into was called the Smoke Room and the other the Third Class Lounge. They were equally uninviting. The Lounge, known as the Steerage, was down below deck, in the bowels of the ship, and believe me, the smell down there left you in no doubt about being in the bowels. If you were a drunken sailor coming home from deep sea or a hardy drover on your way to a cattle sale, or had simply lost the will to live, this was the place for you. Added to the other smells was an overpowering odour of frying fish from a dining saloon which I never had any urge to locate.

The Steerage was quite well furnished, with padded couches round the walls and heavy tables bolted to the floor. As I prayed for death many times during my seasick school journeys, when surroundings and smells seemed immaterial, the same couches offered a comfortable place to suffer.

The Smoke Room was on the main deck and not quite as claustrophobic as the Steerage. It was a smaller room but had wide windows looking out on to the deck and was dominated by a large table which ran the length of the room and took up most of the floor space. There were leather-covered benches against three of the walls and a leather-seated, wooden-armed chair at the other end. I remember this chair because it used to clatter around the room when the crossing got really rough. The smell in there was different. It was a heavy, smoky smell, overlaid with the whiff of beer, as people bought drinks from the bar and drank them in there, and again there was the smell of fish frying in old oil.

On later journeys I found a Non-Smoking Lounge. This was a little bit more inviting, but always full of braying tourists, smoking, with their feet up on chairs to keep the riff-raff out. I can't remember ever using that room.

The journey from Castlebay to Lochboisdale took about three hours on the evening of my escapade and when I wasn't being sick or poking around various rooms I had time to wonder about the wisdom of my actions. The initial rush of defiant excitement had worn off and I had much to worry about. I knew that there was a bus service for boat passengers and I could use it to get from Lochboisdale to Kilpheder, even though I had only a few pennies left. The bus driver wouldn't leave me stranded, on the pier, in the dark, just because I had no money – or would he? And what of my reception at home? I had no doubt that my mother would throw the book and other objects at me when I turned up, having disgraced her with the aunties. I felt that I had been a bit rash, and I had a sinking feeling which had nothing to do with being at sea. Something to do with being nine years old and belonging to nobody.

As the boat came round Gob Na Beinne and the twinkling lights of Lochboisdale came into view, I stood on the deck wishing that I was safe in bed, in Barra. Ben Kenneth gave us shelter and the wind was not as cold as before. Deck hands busied themselves with mops and buckets and families gathered on the deck with their suitcases, peering into the dark for signs of relatives meeting the boat. I didn't bother. Nobody was expecting me.

The voice of the purser came over the Tannoy, 'Will passengers who are disembarking at Lochboisdale and have not yet purchased a ticket please make their way to the purser's office?' A clanging of bells, a whistle or two, and we were there. Soon the boat was tied up and the gangway was put in place. I felt a bit wobbly in the knees as I gave up my ticket, and clinging to the side of the gangway, clutching my bag, staggered down the steep incline, straight into my father.

He gave me a great big hug and it felt so warm. All recriminations were left until later. He just laughed and said, 'You're a wee devil you know! Your mother and these two old relics in Barra have been wearing out the telephone wires since this afternoon. Thank God, you're safe! They'll never make a *caileach dhubh* (nun), out of you' and he laughed again.

My father never really got on with the aunties. He tried very hard, because he was a nice person, but they always viewed him as an interloper who had come from Benbecula and had gained possession of our croft by foul means. I think he was a little in awe of them to begin with and would agree with my mother and them for peace-keeping purposes. However, he told me, later on in life, that he had never been happy about my being farmed off to the aunties at an early age. 'They cooked it up between themselves,' he said, and I believed him. We were very alike, my father and I, and although we had many rows in our day, we loved each other dearly and none of them really counted for much.

When I arrived home I didn't get too big a lecture after all. There was much tutting and shaking of heads from the parents but my father still had a twinkle in his eye. The other children thought I was a bit of a heroine and it was just so good to be home. There were eight of us in the little house now, including my parents, with toddler twins completing the numbers, and the place was fairly bursting at the seams.

I went to the wedding although I was left in no doubt that I was not being rewarded for my irresponsible actions. My mother painted a very vivid word-picture of the awful things which could have happened to me and I took it all to heart. My father said, 'If you ever do it again I'll meet you at Lochboisdale and throw you off the end of the pier.' I didn't believe him. Anyway my mother was going to the wedding and my father said that I could go and keep an eye on her, in case she ran away to Barra. He couldn't go, as one of the cows was sick and the boys were at an age when they wouldn't be seen dead at a wedding. Young though I was, I realised that my father was looking after a sick cow and five children in addition to his usual chores, so that my mother and I could go to a wedding, and that didn't seem fair. But after all, it was none of my business as I didn't live there. The boys asked me to be sure to tell them if I saw any good fights, and I, never having been to an island wedding before, wondered what they could mean by that.

The wedding was the traditional three-day event of the times. The wedding eve was *Latha nan Cearcan*, (The Day of the Chickens). Then there was the wedding day itself. The marriage ceremony usually took place about three o'clock. My father always said that it had something to do with the timing of the Crucifixion. In truth it gave the catering helpers time to ensure that everything was ready for the evening celebrations. On the following day there was the 'house wedding'. That's the direct translation from Gaelic, and as it took place in a house, it will do.

Wedding arrangements up there were fraught with social minefields. First of all you had to invite all relatives, no matter how far-flung. Everyone in your village was invited, as well as everyone in the world who had ever invited you to their wedding. The invitations were for the whole family, and as both sets of parents issued them separately the list was immense. Fortunately, croft work and baby-minding meant that many families attended in relays, and this eased the crowd-control situation a little.

Catering was a miracle. Basically the guests supplied most of the food. Although the invitation did not read 'Bring a bottle', or anything so crass, it could have said, 'Bring a chicken or sheep, and sugar, tea, bread, butter, and a present or money.' So having a large guest list was not half as daunting as you might think. Your guests turned up on the previous day bearing a good share of the catering requirements between them. When I got married on the island, my English mother-in-law to be thought that all the packets of tea and bags of sugar being passed over were to start off our store cupboard. She just couldn't figure out how we were going to keep all the chickens fresh.

Everything to do with the organisation of the wedding reception had its own protocol. Some special people were invited to fulfil a specific function, and it was considered an honour. So, if you had been a waitress, cook, barman or MC at someone's wedding, you left them off your list of helpers at your peril.

Latha nan Cearcan was the day when teams of helpers prepared and cooked the chickens. Sheep would have been slaughtered and prepared for roasting. Domestic refrigerators were a thing of the future, so everything had to be cooked as close to serving time as possible.

This particular wedding was being held at Torlum school in Benbecula, and my mother and I stayed for two days at the home of one of my mother's friends in the neighbourhood. As we took our chickens and other goodies to the bride's house the two old friends giggled like schoolgirls over anecdotes from their carefree days in the living world before they became crofters' wives, or that's what it sounded like. As I listened, that's when I first saw my mother as a person who once had another life. One she now missed.

The scene at the bride's house was one of intense activity. Chickens were being plucked beside a vast mountain of feathers and all the outhouses were being used as temporary kitchens. I remember thinking that the feathers would probably be handy for stuffing pillows or something, and the smell of lamb roasting and chickens boiling made my mouth water. Among the feverish activity men walked around offering tots of whisky to the workers, and judging by the merriment they'd already had a few sips. Barrels of beer and cases of whisky had been laid in for the occasion and when we handed over our bags we were given a chance to toast the forthcoming marriage. You were given a glass (no age discrimination, I was treated the same as my companions). You toasted the bride and groom-to-be, *Slainte Bean 's Fear na Bainnse* (Good health to the bride and groom) and having taken a sip, returned the glass. You were then told to 'have another', meaning another sip, and only the least discerning of the womenfolk would accept, as this could cause 'talk'. We islanders lived in constant terror of causing 'talk'.

A sip from a communal glass was the usual way of serving spirits even among the menfolk. Most households only had one whisky glass, or tot, as they were called. Beer was drunk in the normal fashion, by men only, but although the island had its share of drunks and there were times when a good binge seemed appropriate, I think that the amount of whisky actually consumed by the ordinary people, on a day-to-day basis, was much less than tales of the islands would have you believe. We waited for our turn to eat a 'high tea', with sandwiches, cakes and scones at a table which was constantly being cleared and re-stocked to feed the never-ending stream of laden visitors.

To be truthful, I enjoyed the first day more than the actual wedding day. The high point was the display of presents. A bedroom had been specially set aside for this purpose and the bride's dress hung there surrounded by piles of tablecloths, bed linen, china and all sorts of new household equipment, including innumerable pots and pans. There was no such thing as wedding lists. To even give a hint that you expected presents would be considered the height of vulgarity, so you kept what you needed and I suspect unwanted and duplicated presents were often recycled and used as gifts for other weddings.

We went back to the friend's house and the grown-ups decided that, in the morning, we would not attend the marriage service at Griminish church, which was a fair distance away, as we had no transport. It would be too much walking for me, they said. I think I was being used as an excuse to get out of listening to a long sermon on the joys of procreation, as both my companions had had enough of that.

The wedding itself was a bit of a disappointment. The school was so packed with people that a person as small as I was had a good view of flannel covered knees for most of the evening. There was a lot of noise, with people shouting, trying to make themselves heard above the bagpipes, playing for some brave souls who tried to dance in the spaces left by the crowd. When the time came for the wedding reel to be performed by the bridal party, my mother lifted me on to a chair, so that I could see the amazing spectacle of the bride being whirled off her feet, first by the groom, then by the best man and finally, it seemed to me, by any man in the room. It started off as a Scots reel but was not recognisable for long.

The food was being served in another building and as we went across there we met the bride and groom coming over to join the main party. He had a puffy eye and she had blood on her nice white dress. Apparently some old boyfriend had decided to mark the bridegroom's card and in giving him a thump, had caught the bride on the nose and made it bleed.

Of course fights were always a feature of a good wedding in those days. I think it was taken to mean that you had provided enough whisky; but they didn't, as a rule, involve the bride and groom. We took our leave shortly after that, as my mother and her friend agreed that things could only get worse.

We were not involved in the 'house wedding', as that was usually a smaller function for the helpers, who, having been kept so busy on the previous two days, richly deserved their own special party. As honeymoons were not an island thing, the bride and groom would serve the helpers on this occasion and would have to endure many ribald comments and innuendo relating to their new sleeping arrangements.

So that is how Highland weddings are often reported, as mine was, years later, in the *Daily Express*, as lasting for three days. I did not have to wear my wedding dress and sit there smiling for that length of time. One thing had not changed however. There was a fight, but honeymoons had by then reached the islands, and the groom and I were on our way to Norway, so I didn't get blood on my dress. Now things are different. Some young couples have followed the trend of dispensing with all formalities and living together. Others go to the mainland and get married there. For people who wish to have an island wedding the local hotels and restuarants do the catering and there's no such thing as *Latha nan Cearc*. I'm so glad that I was there, so early in my life, to see it done in the old way.

Chapter Four

HAVING GIVEN ALL AND sundry assurances that I would be a model child for the rest of my time with them, I went back to Barra and the aunties. I think they were feeling a bit guilty about their lack of supervision which had made my escape possible in the first place, and therefore they didn't say too much about it. I was sent back on the boat, like a parcel, in the care of the purser, and I had to sit where he could see me for the entire trip.

I passed the time by listening to some tourists talking about the history of Barra and how that great philanthropist, Gordon of Cluny, had bought it from Roderick MacNeil, the clan chieftain, who had got himself into debt. After he bought it the poor man couldn't work out what to do with it. Colonel Gordon's solution was to offer the beautiful island, home to every species of bird and plant found on all the different islands of the Hebrides, not to mention an indigenous human population, to the Government for use as a penal colony. That man was all heart. I didn't know the exact meaning of the term 'penal', but knew that it was something to do with prisons, and I was glad to hear that the offer had been turned down. That was before I found out about 'Colonel Gordon Nurtures his Purchased People' . . . Part 2, The Highland Clearances.' One of the tourists bought me a glass of lemonade from the bar and was very surprised when I thanked her in English. They probably knew that I was eavesdropping as they moved away from me.

Nothing of much importance happened during my last stretch at the schoolhouse, apart from a fringe involvement as an extra on the film *Whisky Galore*, together with bus loads of other Barra children. I have always believed that I was in the film, but a few years ago, I tried several times, unsuccessfully, to see myself in the old black-and-white movie, in order to show my children; but I think that what I remember as filming may only have been an audition, or perhaps my elbow makes a guest appearance.

As I had never even seen a film, at that stage in my life, I had no particular interest in the stars who converged on the island and had only seen Compton Mackenzie, an imposing bearded figure, a few times from a distance. I knew that he was an important mainlander who loved the islands so much that he bought the Shiant isles and then an acre of Barra, near Tràigh Mhór, the long stretch of white sand used as an aircraft runway, where he had built a house in 1935. As all this had happened before I was born my interest was minimal: I had heard of so many people buying and selling what I thought of as our islands. Compton, however, was spoken of as a good man who had done much for the people and had written a funny book about the 'Polly'. Now it was being put on film and he was going to play a character called Captain

Bunce, but we didn't see him on the set.

Joan Greenwood was there, and also Gordon Jackson, and a huge bearded man whom I later identified as James Robertson Justice. The pseudo Barra accents caused us great amusement and the playground at school next day rang with 'Feenishh offf your composeetions cheeldren.' The ladies all wore enormous amounts of make-up and so, to my amusement, did the men, while the whole filming business was not half as interesting as a trip to the visiting dentist who came to Barra every six months or so.

Mr Louth, the dentist, must have been quite surprised to find the same two little girls in his chair every time he consulted in Northbay. My friend and I had worked out a foolproof way of getting me away from the aunties for the day, by pretending to have toothache. We caught the bus to Northbay and had to present ourselves to the dentist, as an appointment had been made for us. He would pronounce our teeth perfect yet again, and would give us some leaflets and charcoal toothpowder samples. Then we would browse in the post-office shop, have tea in the tearooms and catch the bus back, munching sweets. Eventually the aunties rumbled us and I was forbidden ever to see that friend out of school hours again.

My devious strategies for spending time with children of my own age were born of desperation. School finished at four o'clock and all the other children went home to talk about their school day and complain about the teacher. I went home with the teacher. They soon got to know that if they called at the schoolhouse door and asked if I could come out to play, they were told to go home. No child was ever allowed to go in there. Twice a week I collected milk from our neighbour and was allowed ten minutes for the walk there and back and fifteen minutes playtime with their daughter, my companion in dental deceit. I was timed and sent straight to bed if I was a few minutes late, even if it was only half past six in the evening.

On one occasion, as well as milk, the kind neighbour sent the aunties a sack of potatoes and instructed Maria, his daughter, to help me with carrying it home. As it weighed half a hundredweight our progress across the field, which separated their croft from the schoolhouse, was slow. We speeded up considerably when we saw that a smooth red-haired short-horn bull had detached itself from its harem of cows and was coming after us at a lumbering trot. No matter how fast we ran, mind you, we were still carrying the potatoes. It gained on us and we'd just managed to climb over a fence, having finally dropped the bag, when it caught up with us. To our astonishment, he didn't make any attempt to get over the fence and kill us; he just opened the bag with his stumpy little horns and started to eat the potatoes. We left him to it. The aunties were horrified by our story and forgot to send me to bed for being late. But I was grounded, for most of my final year there, after I rebelled again and caught pneumonia.

Blackberries were the first soft fruit I had ever seen, and a fair distance from the schoolhouse they grew in magnificent abundance. All the local children used to bring me some and asked me to go with them to pick some for myself. I was not allowed to do this. I don't know the reason. I think it had something to do with the locals seeing me and thinking that I wasn't being properly fed. No fear on that score, I was a very chubby child and my brothers used to call me 'Plum Mac Duff'. However, once again I let bravado overcome caution, and I sneaked out to meet my berry-picking classmates. I figured that the game would be well worth the candle.

It was a great experience to pick handfuls of ripe juicy blackberries for the first time and eat them straight from the *druis* (bush). The others, having done this many times, soon drifted off home and I was left there wandering around from bush to bush, until I noticed that it was getting dark and I had no idea where home was. I had the beginnings of a cold and I felt pretty miserable when it started to rain. 'I'll just shelter under this bush for a minute,' I thought; but the next thing I knew it was the middle of the night. I had fallen fast asleep. The rain was now a downpour and I was absolutely drenched.

I staggered out of my shelter and saw some torches in the distance. The aunties had grilled all my known associates and two of the fathers were on their way round the moor, for the second time, searching for me. I can't remember much of the next week or two. My foolishness had cost me dear. I had double pneumonia and have had a weak chest all my life for the sake of a few blackberries.

I can only imagine how frantic the aunties must have been. They took turns sitting up with me night after night, and every time I opened my eyes there was a figure in a chair next to the bed saying the rosary or reading a prayer book. I drifted in and out of consciousness, but apart from feeling as though the *Loch Earn* was sitting on my chest and having a terrible wracking cough, I wasn't in pain – just very confused. Sometimes, in my delirium, I was back home and a toddler again. It was a Sunday, bathed in sunshine and we had been to church and had eaten our dinner. My mother said, 'Let's all go down to the shore and take a picnic with us to eat later.' (The 'shore' was the term we used for the beach.) We walked along the wet white sands and I stopped to look at my footprints, tiny indentations with toes. As I compared them to the larger prints left by my two brothers and the long deep impressions left by my parents' shoes I dropped behind the others. Just then I noticed a rabbit hopping along the edge of the sands, and I ran after it. It hopped a bit and stopped a bit, always just out of my reach. By this time we were halfway up Bruthach 'Ic Ceilieg (MacKellaig's Dune), which to my small puffing body seemed like a mountain made of sand. I felt the tufts of prickly grass scratching my knees as the rabbit disappeared down into a burrow. I followed and was intent on doing an 'Alice in Wonderland' when my father, who had been keeping an eye on me, spotted my fast-disappearing red knickers and dragged me out by the feet.

I experienced that entire afternoon as I hovered between life and death, and it was as clear as day in my fevered mind. As was the other hot summer's day, again in my toddler days, when my father was haymaking on the piece of land behind the house and my brothers and I were looking for bee's nests. (There was a small hillock on that part of the croft where the wild bees sometimes gathered to use its little hollows as hives. When the haymaking began they flew away and left combs of tasty heather honey behind.) As we searched, I could see my mother, coming down the croft, from the house, towards us. She walked slowly and as she crossed the wooden bridge over the stream, we could see that she was holding something, very gently, in her apron, and that she was crying. In her apron were three little ducklings. They had found a small puddle of tar, which my father had dropped when treating some stirks for ringworm and as it melted and shone in the sun, they mistook it for water and had played in it. Stuck together, but still alive, their frightened little voices sounded so sad. After talking to my father and deciding what to do, my mother took them back home and dabbed them with butter to remove the tar, or at least enough to separate them, and she put them in a rag-lined shoe box by our big black stove for the night. By morning two of them had died, but the third survived to become a large drake and chase us round the haystacks.

Strange things happen to your mind when you are very ill and I wondered if the episodes had been a dream as I had no recollection of the events actually happening. However, I checked with my parents and the description I gave of the two days which I had relived were correct in every detail. They said that I couldn't possibly remember them as they had happened too early in my life.

Strangest of all was the night when I was approaching crisis point. Tossing and turning, I looked up to check that auntie was still there, just as she crept through the door with a cup in her hand. As she walked towards me I noticed that her chair was occupied by an old woman who looked straight into my eyes and smiled. She was dressed in black and her head was covered by a fine black wool shawl which crossed over on her chest. The shawl fell open and brushed my cheek, as she leaned over and stroked my forehead and I saw a wedding ring on the middle finger of her hand. The palm felt rough and papery, and the fingers were twisted, but her touch was gentle and cool on my face as I fell asleep.

I thought that someone had come to help auntie with her vigil and did not even mention the old lady to anyone at the time. Years later, after I was married, auntie was visiting us one day and she gave me a little package wrapped in tissue paper. It was my grandmother's ring and as I saw it I knew that I had seen it before. Auntie told me that in the days when her mother got married only the rich could afford a ring of their own, so the priest kept a ring in the vestry which he used for the ceremony and was the bride's only for the day. When the teacher auntie got her first pay-packet she had bought her mother a wedding ring, but by then Grannie's fingers were so twisted with rheumatism that she could only wear it on the middle finger of her right hand. I couldn't wait to ask about the woman by my bedside. There had been no visitors to my bedroom on that night or any other night. My grandmother, another Christina, whom I could barely remember, had never recovered from her broken hip. She was bedridden when I was born and had died shortly afterwards. Auntie was not at all surprised when I told her what I had seen. She said, 'I felt her there, many a night.' I wore that ring on the middle finger of my right hand until recently and have now passed it on to my little American grand-daughter to pass on to hers one day.

When I was slightly better I got the row, but nothing like my just deserts. The housekeeping auntie still sat with me as I recovered. She told me tales of her young days and I got to know her a little better during my convalescence. Poor auntie hadn't been a very bright child at school, or so she maintained, but I think that was due to her frequent absences when croft work demanded it. She had taken her dead brother's place and had worked by my grandfather's side during harvest time. She had a permanent backache which she put down to the rigours of carrying heavy bundles of kelp and bags of peat before her back was strong enough. In a way, I now understand her attitude to my father, as she had kept the croft going, but as a woman she had no rights of tenure.

When she had tried to work on the mainland the only job offered to her was a place on a herring-gutting crew in Lerwick. I can imagine that it was a pretty grim experience for someone as modest and God-centred as she was. Standing on a freezing cold pier with the other fishwives whose humour was not renowned for its sanctity must have been a trial for her. The job itself, taking the guts out of box after box of herring must have been just about as bad as it gets. As she was one of the shorter girls in the team of three her job consisted of beheading, slitting and gutting the herring. The tallest girl could reach the bottom of the barrel, so she got the slightly better job of packing. Auntie was not a very fast gutter, but she told me that it was astonishing how fast some of them worked. Some teams could process thousands of barrels per day, while keeping up a non-stop stream of jokes and banter with the fishermen. She had a deep gouge on the knuckle of one of her forefingers where the sharp *cutag*, a short razor-sharp knife used to slit the herring, had missed its mark. At the end of the first season she had come home, and as her sister, Catherine, had been appointed head teacher at Kyles Flodda school she had joined her as housekeeper.

Auntie Chirsty had a great memory and could recite pages of facts about Nova Scotia, British Columbia, Cape Town, and other places remembered from her school books – facts which came back to me as I visited the places which she knew so well, but had never seen. She told me about the Gulf Stream Drift and its warming influence on our island waters, and as for the life of every Saint who had ever breathed, well, she was word perfect! In her funny squeaky, singing voice, she sang me songs of her own composing, which I'm sure were very deep and meaningful, but her voice was so bad that I couldn't keep my mind on the words; I kept wanting to laugh. In that short period she showed me much love, in her own way.

It was Hallowe'en while I was still an invalid and the children of Barra were celebrating, knocking on doors and daring people to identify them in their disguises. If they were not given a few sweets or a kindly welcome they would take their revenge. Crofters could wake up in the morning and think that it was the middle of the night because their windows had been blacked from the outside. Gates could be removed from their posts and swapped with those from other crofts. (I wondered if that was what happened to the gate from Kissimul castle.) If you were really nasty to the *Gillean Samhna* (Hallowe'en Boys), they would put a *sgrath* (turf) on top of your chimney pot and your morning fire would fill the house with smoke. The schoolhouse was off limits and we never saw *Gillean Samhna* there, but I heard the stories in school. The pneumonia year was different. Teacher auntie invited them all to come and show me their masks and funny clothes. So stunned by this departure from normal procedure were they that they all trooped in and stood by my bedside, in their strange disguises, in total silence. One of them whispered to me, 'We're sorry that you're dying.'

Well I didn't die, I survived and sat my eleven-plus exam nearly a year early. Despite my extreme youth and absence from school due to illness, I passed, and the remaining few months in Barra were a great deal more pleasant. I think the aunties were so relieved that they had survived their task of seeing me through primary school alive that they were in a permanent daze.

Many years later I went back to Barra as a member of a South Uist Concert Party and I was amazed by the number of people who came up to tell me that they remembered me from my days there with the aunties. The warm-hearted Barra folk, I will never forget them.

As a farewell treat, before going back to live with my parents, the aunties decided to take me with them to Glasgow for their annual fortnight's holiday. It was a very exciting experience for me and the aunties did things which they had never done before in their efforts to see that I enjoyed myself. I think they had a good time too.

We stayed with a lady from Skye, whom the aunts had 'found' in the *Oban Times*, a few years previously – a Mrs MacKinnon, who asked me to call her Mistress MacKinnon, and that's how I've always thought of her. She lived on Robson Street in Govanhill, on the second floor of a tenement building. The people in the street had children of my age and I played with them in the close and out the back, by the wash-house, a small brick building with an enormous washing tub, a mangle and a thick odour of boiling suds. The children just absorbed me into their little group as soon as I appeared and we wrote a play which we performed for the people of the street. All who wanted to see it paid a penny and leaned out of their kitchen windows at six o' clock to watch. I think it lasted for about fifteen minutes and all I had to do was shout, 'Scene One' etc., as my new friends said, 'Ony mair an' they wulnae unnerstaun' yer Teuchter accent!', 'Teuchter' being the derogatory term used by Lowlanders for Hebrideans. They were being kind as they didn't want me to be ridiculed. One of them wrote to me for years and invited me to visit her to watch the Coronation on her parents' new television, but my life had moved on even further by then and I had other priorities.

Mistress Mackinnon was always coming up with new things that the aunties should do with me So we went to

Calderpark Zoo and saw huge primates in tiny cages, and I couldn't sleep that night. They took me to the Glasgow Empire to see 'The Logans' and we laughed at the antics of Ma Logan and her son, Jimmy. The beautiful old theatre with its tiered seats and velvet drapes was a wonderland to me, and later on, in my Glasgow student days, I became a loyal patron, when funds allowed. I introduced my student friends to the voice of Calum Kennedy and the comedy of Andy Stewart, and saw Nigel Patrick in *Dial M for Murder*. All thanks to Mistress MacKinnon.

During that holiday, as we walked in the Botanic Gardens and looked at the exotic plants in the glasshouses, the aunties unveiled their plans for our final outing – a day at the Fun Fair on Glasgow Green. I strongly suspected the hand of Mistress MacKinnon in this, as she had heard the other children describe candy floss to me and had seen their incredulous reaction to the news that I had lived so long and had never even tasted it. She had previously suggested to the aunties that they take me to have my hair permed, and the next day I was hanging from wires in the hairdresser's until I was curly. The day after that, half the little girls in the group had theirs done too. 'Keeping up with the Joneses' was alive and well and living in Robson Street.

So, off to Glasgow Green we went and I had my candy floss. I didn't like it then and I don't like it now. We tried to win a coconut and failed, and I had my fortune told by an old woman with a crystal ball. She said that I would spend a lot of my life in buildings with many windows. Maybe she could smell the chalk dust even then. There was much debate about finding a safe ride for me to go on and seeing the 'chairoplanes', hanging, harmlessly, just above the ground, waiting for customers, the aunties decided that this was about my level. They couldn't have been more wrong. That was a lethal ride and as the speed increased and the flimsy swings were whizzing around horizontally, I thought, 'If I survive this I'll never go on a fun fair ride again', and I haven't.

At the end of the holiday the aunties and I took the train to Mallaig and stayed with yet more cousins for the weekend. Mallaig was not very exciting, certainly nothing like Robson Street. I had a girl cousin, a couple of years older than me, but we just didn't have much to say to each other, and she seemed to have a lot of things already planned for the weekend, so I went for walks along the pier with the aunties, smelling the kippery air and dodging the grey and white splots from passing seagulls, waiting for Monday and the boat home.

The journey from Mallaig to Lochboisdale was very, very boring as we watched the islands of Eigg and Rhum and Canna fade into the distance behind us and set off across the Minch for the final lap of our journey to Lochboisdale. I don't think I have ever 'sat still' for so long in my life. I wonder if the aunties had any sad thoughts that their years of responsibility for me would end in a couple of hours? In my youthful selfishness I only felt relief. They kept their thoughts to themselves, and as we parted at Lochboisdale, they transferring to the Barra boat, and I, with my father, catching the bus for Kilpheder and home, we shook hands as usual. No hugs.

Chapter Five

Beanaich an tigh 's na bheil ann	Bless this house and all within
Eadar fiodh is clach is crann	Including wood and stone and beams
Móran bidhe, pailteas aodaich	Plenty of food, abundant clothing
Slàinte dhaoine gu' robh ann.	Good health to those who live therein.

MY BROTHERS HAD LEARNT many verses of the ancient *Duan*, poem, for their part in the Hogmanay celebrations. I just picked it up from listening to them. One thing I had also picked up very quickly since coming back to live full-time in a mixed household was that, on Uist, male and female roles were carved in stone especially at times of traditional celebration, such as Hogmanay.

That night, when darkness fell, my brothers and all the other schoolboys from the village would visit each house in our township, and standing outside the door, they'd chant a poem blessing the house, before being invited in and given bread, scones and cake, fruit of the land, to put in their clean white sacks. My little sister and I stayed at home and helped to prepare the *fuarag* which was to be shared with the *Gillean Cullaig* (Hogmanay boys) when they came to us. *Fuarag* was a mixture of fine oatmeal and thick cream, sweetened slightly with honey. We all had a dip as we prepared it and watched my mother wash her wedding ring and drop it into the bowl. Whichever boy found the ring would be the first to marry. Christmas puddings were not part of our culture but this was a similar thing.

On the island Christmas was not a particularly festive day – just Midnight Mass on Christmas Eve and our socks hung by the stove, to be filled with sweets and odd things that my mother had managed to make for us. War had left the mainland devoid of luxury goods and the island shops only stocked the basics at the best of times. Sometimes if she didn't have enough stuff to fill the sock she'd carve a funny face on a potato and put that in as a joke to fill the gaps. No toys or anything like that. On a treeless island, the custom of having a Christmas tree is a relatively recent one, and in our little thatched house we barely had room for the simplest of furniture, so perhaps it's just as well. Christmas was the the time when you walked down to St Peter's church in the dark and heard the choir singing *Tàladh Chriosda* (The Christ Child's Lullaby) as you knelt by the crib at the church door and saw the baby Jesus at midnight, and that was excitement enough.

This particular year, my first since coming back from Barra, was an exception however. From a cousin on the mainland a parcel had arrived. My mother had sent her two dozen eggs and she had returned the egg-box full of gifts, just before Christmas. Sultanas and spices for my mother (in response to a request), comics for the twins, a comb in a blue leather case for me, and a 'blow football' game to be shared by the three older boys. My father's present was a strange one, but more of that later.

During Christmas week we'd all taken turns, in pairs, playing with the football game, and the two older boys were becoming experts. They all agreed that it was a great thing altogether. With the hustle and bustle of a Hogmanay afternoon underway, our little kitchen was a hive of industry. In a big steamer on the Enchantress stove a large dumpling made with the sultanas and spices bubbled away. The *Fuarag* had been made and put out in the cream shed to keep cool. Scones and loaves of bread were ready for the *Gillean Cullaig* and, for them, my mother had also made a *Strùbhan*, a caraway scone sandwiched between two sweet treacle scones . . . very intricate procedure involving much juggling with the griddle and burning of fingers. First-footers would come late in the evening, and for most of the night the table would be laid and cleared and laid again with the New Year fare. A very, very, busy time for the women of the crofts.

The boys restlessly awaited the coming of darkness, when they could join their friends and get on with the business of going round the houses, chanting their *Duain,* collecting the goodies and dipping into the *fuarags* to see who would be first to the altar. Thankfully the sharing out would be done at another house when the collecting and chanting was finished.

At the sharing house the contents of all the sacks were laid out on a table. One representative of each family took the empty sack to the table and one of the remaining boys was sent outside. The man of the house divided the goods into equal piles, and pointing to each pile at random, would ask the boy outside to name a family. The boy whose family had been named put that pile into his sack, and so on, until each family represented had equal shares. Whatever else we were short of in the New Year even the ducks had their fair share of home-baked goods. The boys loved the old tradition and we all enjoyed the excitement of hearing the chanting at the door and the laughter over the *Fuarag* and the ring. For old people it was a chance to see the young boys of the village and marvel at how they'd grown and squabble about which side of their family they resembled most. It was a very popular custom and the bread was just a useful by-product.

The boys usually went out at about six in the evening and would be home by nine or shortly after. To pass the time, on this particular Hogmanay afternoon, they brought the football game out and started playing it on the large table which stood in the middle of the room. Up and down went the little white ball propelled by gusty blows through the straws.

By this time my mother was getting fairly 'trachled'. The dumpling was nearly ready and as anyone who has baked or cooked for a special occasion can testify, a recipe which produces a perfect sponge for a family tea can turn out a leather pancake if you bake it to impress mother-in-law. My busy mother was anxious, but hopeful. The dumpling was to be the crowning glory of the first-footer's table, and it would have to be just right or it would cause 'talk'. (Causing 'talk' was greatly to be feared in our community.)

Several times during the afternoon my mother, irritated by the shouts of 'Goal!' and hearing us bickering and begging for turns, had told the lads to 'Put that game away, or go and play it somewhere else!'

'In a minute. I can't move now or it will spoil my aim' and excuses like that was the only effect on the boys. They knew that she was busy and pushed their luck.

The dumpling was beautiful. Large, brown and glisteningly perfect in shape. As my mother unwrapped it from its floured cloth and gently manoeuvred it on to her bigggest china plate, a wedding present from long ago, we could see the sultanas dotted around it and the air was filled with the scent of hot mixed spices. 'Well that's that done anyway', said she, as she turned carefully round to put the heavy plate on the dresser and stepped on the little white ball.

Six pairs of eyes were transfixed as she stumbled and the plate crashed on to the stove. She managed to grab the table and steady herself as the dumpling shot up over her head and hit the ceiling before distributing itself among the white sand on the stone floor, in small steaming lumps.

Only my mother moved. She got the sweeping brush and a shovel and swept sand and dumpling off the floor and put it in a pail for the chickens. Then she picked up the 'blow football' game and the little white ball, lifted the lid on the Enchantress stove, dropped it in and in a terrible voice, shouted 'Goal!'

Hogmanay was a time for goodwill, and thinking back I really admire my mother for just carrying on as if nothing had happened. If it had been me, I think the boys may well have found themselves breathing through six feet of earth; well, maybe not, they had lost the game that they loved. They walked on eggshells till the other boys came for them and went to bed very quietly when they came home. I think my mother's lenience stemmed from the feeling that the show had to go on and throwing a few slaps about would only hinder her.

Later, much later that night when the Hogmanay bread had been safely stored and when the first-footers were in full tale-telling flow, we children sleeping in the next room were occasionally woken by a shout of 'Goal!' and gales of laughter as the story was retold. The dumpling was still there 'in spirit'.

First-footing, as most mainlanders remember it, before TV made it a spectator sport, i.e., the lump of coal and 'Here's tae us, wha's like us? Gey few and they're a' deid!', on the stroke of midnight, was the mainland way. In Uist it was different. Our men didn't carry anything but their whisky bottle and some had problems with that. The greeting was, '*Bliadhna Mhath Ùr dhuibh!*' (A Good New Year to you!) and the response '*Mar sin dhuibh fhéin, agus cus dhiubh!*' (The same to you, and many of them!). Again, only the males of the species left the house, while the females got on with the business of seeing that there was plenty of food available.

It wasn't a case of trudging round every part of the village, indiscriminately knocking on doors. Only friends and relatives were visited. You could start as early in the evening as you liked, usually after the schoolboys had had their bit of fun and, breaking off for appropriate reasons like Mass and sleep, it could go on for days. It wasn't considered inappropriate to find a relative from Benbecula visiting you with a bottle and wishing you 'Happy New Year' on January 5th. The 6th being the Epiphany, and another Mass day, seemed to be the cut-off date.

Botul na Bliadhn' Ùire (The New Year Bottle) was the special bottle of good whisky which was taken round the houses. There was usually another left at home, so that first-footers who came in my father's absence could be given a dram from the family. The drams given and received were sips from a communal glass and much of the resulting jollification came from the warm atmosphere generated by good companions in festive mood, funny stories, singing and eating. True, some imbibed more than others and the voices got louder as the night wore on, but by then the sips had become gulps.

We had our regulars, my father's close friends who came to our house and seemed to go no farther, so they were always there at daybreak, hailing the dawn of a new year as the curtains were opened with, 'Oh God, now we've got to go to Mass!' My father made his rounds fairly early in the evening or left it till New Year's Day, preferring to spend Hogmanay at home with the visitors, at least while we were all small children. In those days he was the life and soul of the party. Sadly, much later on in life, after we'd all left home, he got to like the brew too much and after a few mishaps, he went to the priest and took a vow of temperance. So, for many years before his death he was teetotal.

The Mass on New Year's morning was always fairly dramatic and the poor priest tried to keep it short. Some of the men had done the croft work and then stayed up all night making merry, but had managed to stagger to church. The 'holy families' of the parish, as my father called certain members of the congregation, stood out like beacons. Their men were very spruce and looked well rested. Fortunately, they were also the type of people who 'processed' up the aisle to the front seats, genuflected deeply and crossed themselves and said a silent prayer, before gliding into their places. This gave the 'awkward squad', who had not spent the night resting, a chance to shuffle into the back seats, trying to make themselves

61

invisible and as comfortable as the hard pews would let them.

Often there was snoring and other noises which people make in their sleep. It was not uncommon to hear, 'Move your feet', or 'Get me a cup of tea, Mary', being mumbled loudly, but my own favourite memory is of the year when one old man lit his pipe in the middle of the sermon and proceeded to smoke it until his neighbour woke him up.

After Mass there would be the greeting of friends outside the church and hearing the same thing over and over again: 'Thank God this only happens once a year!' But that was not strictly true. There was Games Night and the biggest binge of them all – Cattle Sale Day. This was the day when crofters took their herds to market, and the sorrow of seeing their beautiful beasts go under the hammer – at a fraction of their worth – to the syndicate of dealers with an island monopoly, had to be drowned with some of the proceeds. The outcome was a kind of New Year without the Mass or any other blessing.

For us children, sale day began with the rounding up of the young cattle, which had been fed and watered since their birth with this day in mind. If any of the cows had outlived their usefulness or you needed extra money, they also went. In addition the mare, Sally, produced a foal now and then, and that was an added bonus in many ways. I'll never forget seeing her foals being born and standing up, so fragile and graceful – miniature horses from the first moment of their lives. It certainly beat living with the aunties who treated birth and anything connected with it as unmentionable. Recently my son was present at the premature birth of his own first-born and he described his initial reaction thus: 'I wanted to apologise to this little person for not realising that he'd

been living inside that bump for eight and a half months.'
That's how I felt about the foal.

To get to the sale, the assembled cattle had to be
walked up to Kilpheder cross roads and turned south,
along the main road to Carisheval. It wasn't an easy task,
and for the first part of the trek, or at least until the cattle
got the idea of plodding along the road and not
wandering off into the heather, it was a case of 'All hands
on deck.' We didn't stop to think about the final
destination for our lovely animals and we were certainly
not encouraged to do so; we just herded them along,
occasionally flicking them on the rump with a stick if
they looked like exploring. There weren't all that many
cars on the island at the time and those who owned them
were probably herding their own cattle, so traffic was not
a problem.

Our beasts were pretty complacent as a rule, although
my husband would beg to differ on that score. When we
were first married he offered to help with the cattle drive
on sale day and my father accepted gratefully. Some of
the younger stirks were tethered in a field behind the
house to stop them wandering back down the croft to
their usual grazing ground. As they seemed small and
relatively gentle, more likely to be kind to an English
soldier, he volunteered to bring one of them up to the
road. My father said, 'Well, if you're sure, but whatever
you do, don't let go of the rope or the stirk will be at the
far end of the croft before you can blink.' I don't know if
he had time to blink, but he remembered to hold on to
the rope as the strong little stirk with youth on its side,
felt the smell of freedom in its nostrils and ran like the
wind, round the croft, jumping ditches and trying to get
through fences, only slowing down, now and again, to
aim a kick at his captor.

My poor husband, not wishing to let the side down, had lost his footing in the first few minutes and was dragged like a bundle of rags through clumps of wild iris and thistles, cow-pats and puddles. Over rocks and rough ground and along barbed wire fences, with the blood pumping in his ears he couldn't hear my father bellowing, 'For God's sake man, let go of the rope!' Eventually the stirk ran himself out, and with the honour of the British Army intact (unlike his trousers), my husband was able to drive his exhausted stirk to the sale. The story related by my father to all and sundry resulted in their being treated to many drinks from half-bottles, and my husband came back from the sale convinced that he wanted to be a crofter.

In the old days the same hard core of my father's friends would come back home with him, all having had a few drinks. For us children it was quite exciting. The thought of having a bit more money, although less than expected, always lightened my mother's heart and the visitors would stop off at the shop and buy sweets for us. If we put our money boxes in a place where they could see them, they would put their loose change in there. As we didn't get any regular pocket money we had to seize the day whenever it came. The older children were allowed to stay up a little later and help my mother with the tea as a special favour, and that is how I heard the story of Hector's teeth.

One of my father's friends, who, on similar occasions, came into the house singing *Gruagach Òg an Fhuilt Bhain* (The Fair-haired Maiden) and went from song, to joke, to song, when he'd had a drink, was unusually quiet all evening. At the table he ate little, dipping his sandwich in his tea and making slurping noises. We thought he was just being funny, but he was wincing, not smiling. 'What's up Hector? Not hungry tonight?" asked my mother.

'Well', said Angus, the other friend, 'I think you'll have to find him a bottle with a teat on it. Hector's teeth are sticking out of a bullock's backside!'

Poor Hector had been walking home from the sale and had accepted a lift from a drover. He sat in the back of the truck with four bullocks. The drover was unfamiliar with the island roads and was driving much too fast. At one dangerous bend he didn't get it right and went into the ditch, overturning the truck twice and coming close to killing himself and his cargo. One of the bullocks was killed outright, the others were dazed but unharmed. The driver himself had cuts and bruises, and Hector was knocked out for a few minutes. When he woke up his bleeding mouth was full of coarse brown hair and bits of skin, and at the other end of the truck were his four front teeth embedded in the the rump of the dead bullock. Poor man, in addition to his pain he took a lot of teasing about his fondness for rare beef.

Chapter Six

I HAVE NEVER BEEN PARTICULARLY fond of round-shaped events. You know, flower shows, music festivals, ethnic fairs and such-like gatherings, held out in the open. You seem to cover much ground for very little enjoyment. I think my aversion may have something to do with memories of early Games Days, the big happening of the Uist Summer, which was another round event.

For days beforehand we prayed that the weather would hold, if we were having a warm spell, or that it would change, if it was being its usual blustery self. Many of the exiled islanders earning their living on the mainland booked their holidays to coincide with this week, making accommodation on the ferries even more cramped than usual, as all the islanders who had married mainlanders and settled in Glasgow had the same idea. Mainland pipers and dancers and strong people and fast people and people who wanted to watch the same, doing what they did so well, all crammed on to the *Lochmór* and *Loch Earn* and later on, its slightly less awful successor the *Loch Ness*, on the last boat day before the Games.

As the pipers took advantage of the time to fine-tune their skills in preparation for the competitions, the journey was enjoyable for the Glasgow Highlanders but must have been a nightmare for English tourists, who are not overly fond of hearing a march, strathspey and reel and two different *Ceòl Mór* pibrochs being skirled simultaneously. I am sure some of them thought that the crossing was always like this and vowed never to return.

Games morning, in the glow of memory, was always a sunny one. I think the reason for this could be cancellation in cases of bad weather. I don't know, or perhaps we just didn't go if the weather was bad. The venue was Askernish Machair and a fair step from our house. We walked westward from Kilpheder, down what we called *Rathad na h-Eaglais* (The Church Road), to the wooden bridge over the canal and on past St Peter's church until the gravel road became sandy and we were on Daliburgh machair.

There was quite a good sand road as far as Hallin cemetery, which we skirted after crossing ourselves and saying a silent prayer for dead relatives. My parents always looked sombre at this point and I felt just a little uneasy at the thought of all the dead people lying under the sandy soil, listening to the sigh of the sea close by. Nowadays, when I go there to visit the graves of my father and the aunties, lying closer in death than they ever were in life, I find more of my old friends around me, enclosed by the stout stone walls of Hallin, than in any other part of the island.

As we walked my parents reminisced about friends and family who had died and how the funeral ceremony had changed through the ages. In olden times the whole township closed down to mourn the dead on the day of the funeral and the day after. Not a stroke of unnecessary work would be done and even talk was subdued. This silent time was reserved for praying for the dead and reflecting on human mortality and was not a result of a drunken debauch as A.A. Macgregor would have his readers believe.

The remains of the dead were kept above ground for a minimum of three days, during which time *caithris*, (night watch) took place. This was the custom of sitting in the same room as the dead person day and night, and praying or keeping watch. It was not like an Irish Wake which is more a celebration of the person's life. Family and friends, and indeed the people of the township, would volunteer to take their turn, and having done it myself a few times I can testify that sitting in a room with a corpse at three in the morning makes you very much aware of your own eventual destiny.

In even earlier times the funeral cortège left the house of the bereaved and moved southwards through the township of Kilpheder, then turned westward to Kilpheder machair and proceeded along the shore until they arrived at Hallin cemetery. My father referred to this as '*A leantal cuairt na grèine*' (following the journey of the sun). The priest would conduct a service at the graveside, but the coffin was not actually taken into the church at all, as it always has been for as long as I can remember. *Coisgeas* (refreshments), the literal translation is 'expenses', consisting of biscuits and cheese and a small dram, were offered to the mourners outside the cemetery wall after the burial, and this dates back to the time when people came from as far away as Eriskay to bury their dead in Hallin. It was a custom born of necessity, as the funeral party would have crossed the Sound of Eriskay to

Ludag by boat, and then would have walked for hours, taking it in turns to carry the coffin along the traditional route towards Hallin cemetery.

Beyond the cemetery and one of the best trout-fishing lochs in Uist we walked on and on, the road becoming more of a track where it was used by crofters to drive their tractors and carts at harvest time. After what at that time seemed to me like three days, we could hear the skirl of the pipes and knew that we were nearly there.

The perimeter of the games arena was defined by stout poles and rope barriers and all around the circle were parked an assortment of vehicles, a couple of buses and lorries, some cars, vans and even the odd tractor. There were some large marquee-type tents for the judges and for the committee, and of course teas and beer. Several events were going on at the same time and I didn't have any interest in 'putting the shot', 'tossing the caber', or wrestling. Pibroch to this day leaves me cold and even the jollier reels and jigs paled after a time.

I kept losing sight of my parents, and after a while, once I got used to the crowds and found some of my friends, that was fine. We wandered around and watched some of our more nimble schoolfriends dancing the highland fling and sword dance, kilts flying, on the wooden platform, until that got boring. Eventually we made our way past the clusters of men drinking and talking behind the vehicles down to the sand dunes, where we played sliding games and held our own dancing competition. We all knew the steps and agreed that we were as good as any of the competitors.

When we got back to the games the junior sports events were in full swing and they were just announcing the girls' flat race. Well now, this was our chance to participate, and we all took our shoes and socks off and lined up. After a few false starts we heard the official shout: 'Ready, steady, GO!' and we were off. It was over one hundred yards and fairly early on I realised that I was out in front, as I could not see anyone running beside me, so I carried on running as fast as I could. Just ahead stretched the finishing line, so I thought, 'I'll just look to see where the others are' and slowed down to do this while the rest of the field shot past me. So ended my career as a promising athlete. My brothers, who had been watching in amazement, did not let me live that down for a long, long time.

The tea tent was presided over by Mrs Lindsay, a distant relative of ours, and was always doing good business. Long folding tables and planks of wood stood on trestles inside and a never-ending stream of people were served buttered scones and sandwiches, currant cake and biscuits, and tea poured from huge kettles wielded by perspiring helpers. If the day had turned chilly as so often happened on the machair, so near the Atlantic, a hot cup of tea and somewhere warm to sit were very welcome indeed. Any of us who went in could depend on the ties of family to ensure that our portions were very generous.

Occasionally some of the younger children, escaping from the restraining clutches of their parents and becoming bored with the entertainment on offer, would get up to mischief, such as sticking pins through the canvas of the tea tent, to the consternation of the *cailleachs* (old ladies) who were seated next to the canvas. Joan, the proprietrix, would run out shouting and brandishing a tea towel, but the culprits would show a clean pair of heels, knowing that she could not desert her post.

As the presentations took place immediately after each event the successful competitors were free to walk around showing off medals and cups, and in some cases spending prize money in the beer tent. One young piper, Donald Morrison, then a mainland policeman, always took time to seek my parents out and have a bit of banter with them. He loved to hear the satirical verses that my father composed about happenings on the island in his own absence and urged him to do more recording. At that time crofting and seaweed were as much as my father could fit into his life and ceilidhs which passed the winter evenings were his only platform. To me Donald Morrison was the most gorgeous man I had ever seen. In his full Highland dress, carrying an armful of trophies, his tall blonde figure made me think that if Michael the Archangel ever fell to earth he'd look exactly like Donald Morrison. My adoration took the form of gaping at him open-mouthed while hanging on his every word and still trying to think of some way of catching his attention as he said his usual farewell to my father: 'One day, Norman, we will both be famous and I'll compose a pipe tune in your honour.' Donald went on to win most of the piping contests world-wide, becoming Pipe-Major of the Police Pipe Band, playing for Royalty and even having his picture on beer cans. I think the latter achievement more than any other impressed my father. Until one day a good twenty-five years after the games of long ago, when he was listening to a piping programme on the radio and the announcer said, 'Now we have Pipe-Major Donald Morrison playing his latest composition, the march, *Norman MacMillan of Kilpheder*. My Archangel had kept his promise to his old friend.

And so, Games Day would draw to a close. The last event, usually being a tug o' war between the North End men and the South End men. As my father came from Benbecula in the far north and my mother from

Kilpheder in the south I was never sure which side to shout for; but whichever team won, I could not lose.

As we walked home along the machair road, past the cemetery, now looking even more lonely and forlorn, we were often a much larger group, with friends and neighbours from the village all walking together, talking over the events of the day. Again the cemetery evoked talk of the dead and ghost stories. Someone mentioned that an elderly man from Daliburgh was talking of building a house on the machair near the cemetery, and we all agreed that he had more courage than any of us. One of the group joked that Calum would be able to fish Loch Hallin as often as he wished and his neighbours would not be able to report him to the bailiff. Although we all laughed I can remember shivering at the thought of spending a night near the cemetery walls. The house was built, and the old man lived quite happily there for many years; if he ever saw any ghosts he didn't tell us. Conversation became more general as we got back to the gravel road and the length of the Hebridean summer's day being what it is we arrived home long before dark.

I mentioned Games Night as one of the binge nights, but early in my life it was pretty quiet for our family. After walking the machair road twice in one day and all the activity in between we were all very tired and knocked out by the fresh sea air. We children would be asleep before our heads touched the pillow. Our parents likewise. They had spent the day meeting old friends, some of whom they had not seen since last Games Day, enjoying the spectacle of the dancing and other activities in a way that we children had yet to learn, and they were pretty tired themselves.

Occasionally a passing reveller would knock at the door offering a dram, and however late the hour, he would be admitted, given a cup of tea and listened to until he could be persuaded to go home. It was not the done thing in Uist ever, ever, to let a knock on your door go unanswered.

As we got older we discovered that Games Day did not end with a weary trudge back home on the machair road. There were dances to go to: dances that were considerably enlivened by the presence of all the young pipers, dancers and athletes who had come to the island to compete at the games.

The main venues for the dances were the gym, in Benbecula, so-called because it had originally been used as an RAF gymnasium in the days of 'the airmen', then used as a community hall, and also the Territorial Army drill hall in Daliburgh. There were also dances at some of the schools in other areas, Garrynamonie and Eochdar in particular, and much later, when the North Uist causeway was in place, we would venture as far afield as Cairinish and Lochmaddy. But that was still in the future.

The accepted age for such a mature practice as going dancing was fifteen at the earliest. You could go to weddings with your parents and even join in the dancing there and we used to have end of term parties at school where my eldest brother would play the piano for a bit of Scottish dancing. As for real dances we were all too young for that for some time. Also in the future, on the day which I have just described, were two games nights which will live in my memory forever. They both began with a knock at the door, but there the similarity ends.

The first knock concerns someone coming with news of yet another Donald. He was the young son of our nearest neighbours, a very hard-working young man and not one to get drunk or cause any trouble. Well liked by all who knew him, he had a passion for vehicles and knew his way round any engine. On Games Night he was coming back home in his lorry when the driver of a jeep, whose vehicle had broken down, stopped him and asked for assistance. He was about to tow the vehicle to the nearest layby, off the narrow single-lane road of the time and was tying the tow-rope under it when tragedy struck. The brake slipped and the jeep rolled on top of him, killing him instantly. It took a long time for many people to get over the horror of that night.

The second event concerns my husband (the English soldier of stirk-catching fame). We were stationed in Benbecula at the time, before taking off for far-flung places and had come down to the games with our toddler son. We combined the day with a visit to my parents and stayed the night at Kilpheder. My mother, the little one and I all went to bed fairly early. My father went out to the post-box at Kilpheder crossroads to post a family birthday card which had been forgotten due to games excitement and preparations for the granchild's visit. Only my husband was there by the fire, reading the usual day-old paper and finishing a cup of tea, before going to bed, when he heard a loud knocking at the door.

Thinking that it was my father pretending to be a Games Night drunk, he opened the door with a suitable greeting at the ready. It was a Games Night drunk, Peter, a very short fellow from the village, who could be relied upon to get plastered on every special occasion and others in between. He had a sorry tale to tell, and as he made himself comfortable he produced a half-bottle of whisky and proceeded to share it with my husband, whose first thought was, 'If we finish this bottle quickly, he'll go and I can get to bed.' It appeared that Peter and some others had been drinking at Polachar Inn at the far south end of the island. When closing time came they got a lift home in Willie Jordan's car. He lived in Kilpheder and it was all very convenient. However when they got to the crossroads instead of turning left towards Kilpheder village, Willie had driven into the ditch.

This happened from time to time with Willie, so my husband was not unduly concerned as Peter seemed to be in fine form. He was concerned however when Peter, having finished the first half-bottle, produced a second one from another pocket. Thinking that a hasty dispatching of the contents would also dislodge Peter, he was past caring when a third was produced. Halfway through the fourth, it crossed my husband's addled brain that he had not heard of this man as being a generous person. On the contrary, he was known to have short arms and long pockets and would cadge a drink off anyone if he could. 'All lies', he thought as he eventually shut the door behind Peter and tried to find his way to bed.

Before he'd got very far my father came back. 'Sorry to leave you alone for so long,' he said, 'I was giving some people a hand. Their car had been ditched out by the post-box and they were in one Hell of a state.'

'Were many of them hurt?' asked my husband, shocked into semi-sobriety.

'Not a scratch on them,' said my father, 'but when they got the car out of the ditch all their half-bottles had disappeared and I've been helping the poor fools to comb the ditch for them, but no joy.'

One of the reasons I remember that night is that after he had been sick for the third time, my husband decided that he didn't want to be a crofter. I don't know if justice ever caught up with Peter, but if it did I'm sure that he had a very plausible alibi, ready to cover his back.

Chapter Seven

COMING HOME FOR GOOD had been a dream for such an eternity that when it eventually happened it seemed like an extended holiday for a long time. Paradoxically, what I liked best and disliked most was being surrounded by the other children in the family. For years I had longed to be able to play and talk with children of my own age and this I could now do at will. However, there was a downside – they just never went away.

I woke up in the morning and they were there, all day and until nightfall there they were, and when we got ready for bed I had to share a bed with my sister. We slept in the small room called the closet. That gives a good indication of its size. It also served as a bathroom on Friday nights when the zinc bath came out along with the worm syrup and the syrup of figs. The larger bedroom had three beds – one double for my parents, and two singles, each with one boy at the head and one at the foot. Scathing comments have been made by present-day do-gooders about such sleeping arrangements leading to all sorts of incestuous behaviour among the peasants. Take it from me, it was all about fighting for control of the blankets and getting away from smelly feet.

Having lived in solitude for so long, I'd grown used to amusing myself and being quiet and studious for most of the time . . . I'd had no alternative. Now it seemed that there was no such thing as my own space. Our little house was seething with fast-growing bodies. Those who had lived there all their lives had not even noticed it, but sometimes it just closed in on me.

At the south end of the house stood my father's old cart, which, although he now had a tractor, was kept handy, as it was more suitable for hauling crops and peat from the less accessible parts of the croft. Its long wooden shafts lay along the ground and the green and white wooden box resting at an angle against the wall of the house became my sanctuary. I'd go in there when I wanted to be alone, to read or just to think. Once I fell asleep there, dozing in the sun, until one of the other children was sent to look for me and saw the dog, another Scot, sitting by the cart. After that, they always knew where to find me.

The aunties, who had many times wished themselves free of 'other people's property', meaning me, must have felt the need for more good works to offer up to God. Either that or they felt lonely on their return to Barra, as they asked my mother to bring the twins over for a visit. They went over with my mother on a Friday. She returned on the Monday and the twins came back to the croft to stay three years later. We just accepted it, together with my mother's assurances that the little ones had insisted on staying as they were having such a good time. We just got on with sharing the extra space. The aunties had mellowed somewhat and the twins were company for each other, but as I found out recently, it was a lively household and not always a happy one. The task proved too much for the aunties and they sent Alick back six months before his twin, causing her much anguish, but that is not my story to tell. I missed my dainty little sister, with her will of iron, and the serious little boy who would fight dragons to protect her. As their return home coincided with my departure for six years of further education in Fort William and Glasgow, and they had left home by the time I came back to Uist as a teacher, we were all adults before we really got to know each other. I wonder about the wisdom of it all, but again I suppose it was all about survival. School was about to start and I had much on my mind.

Daliburgh School was on two sites at the time. The old corrugated-iron building by the loch, near Daliburgh crossroads housed the academic section, composed of pupils like myself and my two older brothers, who had passed the eleven-plus examination. About a quarter of a mile further south, again by a loch, stood the technical school, where, if the examiner who had marked your paper had not had a good day and failed you by one point, you studied woodwork and domestic science instead of Latin and algebra.

We were indeed blessed by the quality of our teachers. Take that from the horse's mouth. I hated some of them, but they knew their subjects and could teach them, and at the end of the day that is what it's all about. Some of the teachers came from the island and a few were recruited from the mainland. The incomers lived with their families in the newly-built Swedish houses on the Daliburgh/Lochboisdale road.

I can't, honestly, hand on heart, say that I enjoyed my time at Daliburgh school. I was a very small fish, in a vastly wider pool than that to which I had been accustomed. Add to that the fact that my two older brothers had been spawns of the devil at school since joining the infant department. Although clever, even gifted, as later life revealed, they were involved in every prank played on the teachers throughout the school and had been belted so often that it no longer hurt. Donald John, a budding poet, specialised in composing stingingly accurate but uncomplimentary Gaelic verses about the mainland teachers and circulating them in class. He got away with it for a long time as he told the teachers, who couldn't read Gaelic, that it was homework, but he wrote one about a local teacher once, got caught and that was the end of that, and nearly the end of him. He had trouble writing anything at all for a few days. Fortunately it didn't extinguish his love of verse and up to the time of his early death at the age of forty-eight he had songs recorded by well known Gaelic singers and poems well received at mòds, the Gaelic Festivals.

Because of the closeness of our ages and my being almost a year ahead of my peer group plus the fact that it was a rural school, we often shared the same classroom. To some of the teachers I was just going to be another problem, and they said so the first time they called the register, with such comments as, 'Not another MacMillan! Well I hope your brothers have told you that we stand for no nonsense here.' Later in life I shared a staffroom on equal terms with some of the people who had given me that rousing welcome to the most important part of my education, and I was tempted to tell them that they had done me a favour; they had taught me what I should never, never say to a new pupil, and I never did, I knew how much it could hurt. However, they were good colleagues, and I hope that by that time they had learned to judge me on my own merits. My brothers were certainly not unhappy about their notoriety, I was only one year behind them in educational terms, but many, many years adrift in terms of real life.

The school took pupils from all over the island, and also from Benbecula and Eriskay. If you'd passed your exam transport was provided, and in the case of children from Benbecula and Eriskay, lodging expenses were covered. Benbecula had its own junior secondary schools, but if parents from that area wished to send their children to Daliburgh they could do so. It meant that I was not the only new face on my first morning and this helped me to settle in and make friends.

Despite the influx from feeder schools, classes were small and combined, to bring the numbers up. It was not easy for the teachers, as planning for a small mixed group is much more difficult than teaching a larger class, where the age and ability playing field is level. Despite this we had a very good education and although, or perhaps I should say because, the discipline was very strict and the belt always a reality, many of us went on to further academic studies from that little corrugated iron school by the loch.

The headmaster, true to the tradition of the times, was a newly-appointed mainlander and although he wasn't cast in the mould of some previous headmasters who made a name for themselves by consorting only with island aristocracy and throwing gifts to the natives, he had no knowledge of the language or the culture. Still, he liked the island, wore a cloth cap, and in time learned a little of our ways.

After a year at the school we had grown to respect him as a fair man and someone who knew his teaching subjects well. However, one thing which had obviously been preying on his mind since experiencing his first Hogmanay was the imminent arrival on his doorstep of a little gang of *Gillean Cullaig*, chanting and expecting something for their flour sacks. So he decided to do something about it, not recognising that this ritual had been in place for generations and that the *Duain* were a gem of Gaelic culture passed on by word of mouth throughout the years, which without annual usage would be lost. The *Gillean Cullaig* were as much a part of Uist tradition as Ben Mór was part of our landscape.

Before the end of the autumn term the Headmaster announced, 'There will be no Hogmanay begging this year.' He had summoned the whole school before him to deliver this announcement, and he followed it by inviting any boy who intended to defy his ruling to step forward. Naturally, my brother Donald Angus took it upon himself to put his hand up and say, 'Please Sir, it isn't begging.'

'And will you stay at home?'

'No, Sir!'

Donald John had become a bit more worldly-wise since his exposure over the the poetry incident and kept out of this little drama.

'Then, step forward and hold out your crossed hands!'

So, the headmaster proceeded to administer a brutal punishment for something which was not in any way connected with school work and was going to take place during the school holidays. This illustrates the attitude of some of the mainlanders. They were there not just to teach us but to civilise us.

After six hefty strokes the question was repeated again, and again the same answer was given. Someone in my class told me that the total number of strokes was twenty-four. I didn't count them. I never could stomach blood sports and was silently crying my eyes out behind my hands. My brother would not change his answer, and so he was sent home, in disgrace, for the rest of the day.

It says much for the total trust that island people had in the infallibility of teachers, doctors and priests, that the reaction my parents showed to that incident was to tell my brother, 'That'll teach you to be cheeky to your teachers. Shame on you!' Years later, when I was teaching at the school I came across the personal files on the twins, who had left the school by then, and human nature being what it is I had a peek. In the space for general comment it read: 'As with the rest of the family, no parental interest shown.' It made my blood boil! No parents could have been more interested in their family's welfare, but unlike some who were always beating a path to the school door, my parents trusted the teachers to know their jobs and unless specifically asked to go to the school, they left them to get on with it.

The brother who had been punished was the pianist, and the Christmas party wasn't the same that year, as his hands were still so swollen that he couldn't play for the dancing. The *Gillean Cullaig* were, if anything, more in evidence than ever that year, but in Daliburgh, they gave the schoolhouse a wide berth, and after New Year, when the new term started, the subject wasn't even mentioned. I wonder if one of the local teachers had had a quiet word with the headmaster. Someone had obviously straightened him out.

Some of the teachers and the headmaster taught in both the academic and technical school and spent a lot of time either walking or cycling between the two sites. Some of us pupils also had the opportunity to take this bit of exercise. If one of the female teachers had decided to belt anyone and they thought that their lighter, more lady-like straps were not fitted to the severity of the crime, the culprit would be told to walk to the other school and borrow the headmaster's strap, a quarter-inch thick 'Lochgelly'. Not a nice trip! You didn't mind the walk; it was the indignity of going into a classroom full of your peers and making the request, then walking back carrying the strap and meeting shoppers and other road users who knew exactly was going to happen to you, that made it hatefully humiliating. Yes, I speak from experience. After receiving your punishment, you took the strap back. The good old days.

There was little in terms of organised after-school activities, especially for the girls. A boy's youth club was started once and my brothers really enjoyed that. They learned how to make plaques from plaster of Paris and how to play some new card games, but for some reason funding was withdrawn and the club closed. We had a very keen music teacher at the school. A mainlander, his main subject was science, and although all he taught us about music was the joy of memorising every song in the *Oxford School Song Book* and singing them in harmony, it gave us a lot of pleasure. I can still hear my brothers and their friends coming home from the youth club singing 'Swing Low Sweet Chariot' and 'The Song of The Volga Boatmen', their young male voices carrying on the clear Hebridean air. We could hear them coming from over a mile away, as they walked home in the moonlight.

Once a year a teacher from Skye came to get us ready for the local Mod, a daunting task, as she had one school term to tour all the schools on the island, from Benbecula southwards. She taught choral harmonies, duets and solos for all different age-groups and tutored us up to competition performance standards for the big day.

Although I enjoyed some success later in life, my own attempts at competitive singing at the Daliburgh Mòd were pathetic. I had never sung in public before and was so nervous that all I wanted to do was finish the wretched song and get off that stage. My mother said that she had never heard a lament sung so fast in her life. As I was singing I could see Miss MacDonald, the teacher from Skye at the back of the Hall shaking her head in disbelief; when she covered her face with her hands I knew that the gold medal was not for me.

The household chores were still shared out and I had my own bits and pieces to do, but there was plenty of time allowed for homework and any other activity we wanted to become involved with. I joined the church choir along with some other young girls and that was nice. Singing and music of any kind was just always there in our family. My father was becoming established throughout the islands as a singer and comedian of some repute. He had people from The School of Scottish Studies coming regularly to record his enormous repertoire of traditional folk songs and Francis Collinson and later on Fred McAulay of the BBC often invited him to Glasgow to take part in Gaelic programmes.

Born ahead of his time as many people are, he received some recognition during his lifetime and that was enough for him. In the 1960s, when he helped Arthur Swinson with the research for his most enjoyable book *Scotch On The Rocks*, the author described him as . . . 'possessing a voice full of fire and richness' and . . . 'one of the most straightforward and most reliable men I have ever met in my life.' That meant more to my father than money in the bank.

My mother also had a melodious voice and had once won a silver medal at the Mòd, but she had grown to dislike like performing in public. She loved her piano which had been bought for her by the teacher auntie as a sweetener when she came home from the mainland, and it stood next to the dresser for as long as I can remember. She and Donald Angus would compete to see who could play the fastest, most note-perfect reel with their left hand, whilst covering their eyes with their right hand. Then young Donald started playing, and he was just as proficient but preferred the accordion. Donald John liked to write alternative, often unprintable, words for the songs, and I practised my listening skills and joined in the singing. So, like many of the island folk we were all born with music in the blood, so to speak, and one of the joys of going back to live with the family was having music of one kind or another around me, all the time. On a Sunday night we would listen to The Top Twenty on Radio Luxembourg and try to scribble the words to 'Tennessee Waltz' and other popular songs, so that we could sing them at playtime in the school shelter, much the way every little girl wants to be a Spice Girl nowadays: nothing changes all that much.

In the third year of secondary school we were all getting more fashion-conscious and I decided, in my spare time, to become an agent for a mail order catalogue, or 'club book' as we called them in those days. I risked ticking the over-18 box, and got away with it. It was a very rewarding venture in terms of meeting people and taking their orders, and I enjoyed the very simple accountancy involved, but really I needed much larger orders than my twenty members could afford in order to clothe myself from the proceeds.

Many of my clients were the people who had moved into the Swedish houses in Daliburgh. In fact the wife of a mainland teacher at the school was a very good customer. I always timed my visits to her when I knew he'd still be at school or on a Saturday morning when he had some extra classes. I thought he just might find it embarrassing to have a pupil collecting money from his wife. She must have been a very lonely person, as she always greeted me like a long-lost friend of her own age and gave me tea and cakes. We had long conversations about clothes and furniture and other more personal things. She asked my advice on many things and I found this extremely flattering. Some of my school friends lived near them and told me that Margaret was a very formidable lady and that she and her husband had rows which the whole neighbourhood could hear. I said that I had found no evidence of this and defended her stoutly.

One evening I was later than usual making my collection and when I knocked on the teacher's door I heard the sound of something being thrown against the wall and glass breaking. The door flew open and my teacher rushed out, looking distinctly nervous. He pulled up short when he saw me on the step. From the kitchen came Margaret's voice, screeching in fury, 'Get out of my sight, you useless, bald-headed, skinny-legged bugger!' Need I add that he put his hand in his pocket, pulled out a wad of money, paid their account off, and told me that my services would no longer be required. I don't know which of us had the redder face. I think he had. I made no mention of the incident at school or at home. She had been nice to me and I owed her and him their dignity.

Another customer was a little, old, local lady who lived by the canal. She was a little ball of a woman, who talked incessantly and could knit faster than anyone I've ever known. She often visited us, walking up the canal path and over the bridge, knitting a sock for one of her sailor sons as she went, and on many occasions, leaving

the ball of wool behind in her cottage. One of us had to
follow the trail of wool back there and do battle with her
current 'bad dog' to retrieve it.

She and my father were forever teasing each other.
When we had the Christmas parcel containing the ill-
fated 'blow football' set, my father's gift was a pair of
joke spectacles with nose and moustache attached. This
kind of thing was a complete novelty at the time, and
right up his street. He'd put them on to tell the twins
stories when they came over from Barra for the school
holidays and have them laughing so much that they
begged him to stop. One day he happened to have the
disguise in his pocket as he was passing Mary's house. As
the door was open he could see that she was doing
something over at the dresser with her back to him. So he
quickly put the spectacles on and with nose and
moustache in place, knocked on the door frame to attract
her attention. Mary greeted him politely with 'It's a fine
day' in English and '*Có an aimn Dhé, a tha seo?*' (Who,
in God's name is this?) in Gaelic. Like most elderly people
who live alone, she talked to herself. My father explained
in his poshest English that he was one of her daughter's
friends from Oban, touring the Islands, and had called to
see her, as her daughter had said that she made a very
good cup of tea and was always glad of company.

Mary sat him down and continued to be very polite to
him in English, while calling the wrath of God down on
her daughter's head for sending mainland visitors to eat
the little food she had in the house, in Gaelic, and started
brewing the tea. The light in the little cottage was always
dim, as she used the sill of the small window as an extra
shelf and had a very large geranium plant sitting there.
When she poured the tea she asked, 'How much sugar do
you take?' adding, '*Tha mi'n dòchas gu'n tachd e thu*' (I

87

hope you choke on it), in Gaelic. My father, who had whipped off the spectacles answered, in his own voice, '*Dà spàin, ma 's 'ur toil, a Mhàiri*' (Two spoonfuls please, Mary.) She got the tea towel and started to beat him about the head with it till he had apologised to her satisfaction. Later she saw the funny side and they both had a good laugh.

When I started going round with the catalogue I took the canal path, as it was a good short-cut to the main Daliburgh/Kilpheder road. I had been passing Mary's door for a few days before she noticed me, and called me in for a glass of *Leann nam Biast* (Worm Beer), a drink which she brewed in a large, glass sweet jar and kept on her dresser. It was made from beremeal, a kind of barley, treacle, sugar and water which fermented and produced a fizzy light brown drink not unlike a light ale. The grains at the bottom of the jar grew fat and flabby as they absorbed the liquid and as they moved around during fermentation looked just like maggots – hence the name. The process of topping up with sugar and treacle to keep the supply going was known as 'feeding the worms'. While I sipped my drink Mary took a good look at the catalogue and exclaimed at the variety of goods on offer. She was very interested and decided to spend ten pounds on something. Now she lived in a tiny cottage and had no mod. cons. whatsoever, so I expected her to order a new kettle or something really practical, but no, she turned to the fashion pages and ordered a very classy-looking blue crêpe de Chine dress with a cream silk shawl collar, for considerably more than ten pounds. As I had never seen Mary in anything other than a black or brown jumper and black skirt with a flowered overall covering most of it, I assumed that she was buying a present for one of her daughters.

A couple of weeks later I ran into her some distance from her cottage, stacking peat on the bog. As she had a bag filled ready to carry home I offered to take it and leave it by her door. She accepted my offer and as I was about to take my leave I asked her if the dress had arrived. 'Yes, indeed, and I am well pleased with it!' she said, taking off coat, cardigan and the overall to display the blue dress in all its glory. I'm sure it was the only model of its kind which had ever been worn to stack peat, but from that day on I knew that Mary, despite age and outward appearances, had the soul of a young girl. We became good friends and she taught me many things, including how to turn the heel of a sock. She was old enough to be my grandmother, but that didn't matter; and when, during my time at Fort William school, my parents wrote to tell me that she had died suddenly, I felt that someone very special had gone from my life.

Chapter Eight

THE ISLAND WAS CHANGING, many new ventures were taking shape and the tourist industry was taking its first tentative steps. Due to the excellent fishing in all the lochs South Uist had always enjoyed the patronage of the fishing and shooting set, mostly friends of the people who owned the island. We had grown up with the spectacle of tweed knickerbockered, deerstalker-hatted strangers pulling up outside our house and creeping over our fields, shooting at flying things. The islanders worked their crofts, but at the end of the day the landlords owned crofts and tenants. Now with the the story of the 'Polly' immortalised on film and travel through the island becoming less arduous we actually had people without guns and fishing rods visiting our island.

The hotels smartened themselves up and built cocktail bars, and although to go in there more than twice in a year could still 'cause talk', if you were a woman, liberation was on its way. The new 'Co-op' in Daliburgh had fresh-baked bread delivered three times a week, so a lot of the wives baked their final scone.

My own favourite innovation was the coming to Uist of the tupenny ha'penny bun. Again pioneered by the Co-op bakery this was actually the name used to classify a selection of sweet iced buns with toppings of sticky icing and sprinkles of hundreds and thousands, little bakewell tarts, apple tarts and the unforgettable fly cemeteries, a pastry sandwich filled with a mixture of deliciously blended dates and currants which looked just as their name implied. We could walk up to the shop in the school lunch-hour and spend our pennies in style. Much time was lost dithering over choices, but it was always worth it. For those of us with a cash-flow problem there was the less appealing poor relation, the penny bun. This was an ordinary sweet unadorned currant bun and better than nothing. Unlike the present-day shopping magnates who are driving the small grocer to the wall, the improvements in the Co-op were immediately followed by marked improvements in the other shops, so we the customers were the winners, or at least so we thought at the time. Now, on the island most of the milk, bread and coal come from the shops, while acres of arable land lie fallow and cows are conspicuous by their rarity, as are peat stacks. Perhaps the advent of the tuppeny ha'penny bun wasn't such a good thing for island culture after all.

In my schooldays milking the cows was my mother's exclusive domain, and it always had been. I had tried it once or twice but they didn't want to stand still for me, and my father said that when they saw me coming, with my long nails, they ran screaming to the other end of the croft. In the winter when the cows were in the byre it was easy to get round them in a short time, but once the weather lightened my mother would walk down to the far end of the croft and milk them where they grazed. They knew her well and always stood still, with no need for a *buarach* (tether), just chewing the cud, flicking at flies with their tails and nuzzling her shoulder from time to time. If she was ill or had to go out somewhere at milking time my father would take her place, and the cows accepted him as a substitute, as he sang to them and he was the one who delivered their calves.

One evening both my parents were out and the task of milking was left to Donald Angus, as he had helped out from time to time. Off he went with the pails and all went well until he approached Letty, a cow of some character, who had been with us for a long time and was very attached to my mother. Letty took one look at him and decided that this person was not going to get a drop of milk from her. Every time he got near her she walked off. Eventually she stopped and he hunkered down with the pail between his knees and got started. All went well until Lettty turned her head and nuzzled his shoulder. At once she remembered that this was not the usual milkmaid and she was off again, taking the pail with her and leaving him lying on the ground covered with milk. Not one to give up easily, my brother came back home, camouflaged himself by putting on my mother's milking coat, covered his head with one of her scarves and off he went again. This time he had complete success. Letty thought that her own dear friend had returned and gave him a pailful of milk. He was coming back in, just walking round the end of the house with the pails when Donald MacKellaig, one of his friends, passed by on his bike and called out, 'Hello Kate!' Letty was not the only one who had been fooled. Donald Angus rushed in and dumping the pails on the floor announced, 'I'll kill any one of you who tells him that it was me.'

Donald Angus and Donald John missed the youth club but they were growing up now and in their final year at

Daliburgh school. They were always full of schemes for making money. Fishing was not an option as it was too slow a sport for their liking. Although they tried the canal occasionally they soon got tired of waiting for a bite and started catching eels instead. This had no useful end-product as eels have never formed any part of the island diet, and the whole thing was quite disgusting. They'd wait for an eel to slither through the mud at the shallow part of the canal, spear it with a fork and cut its head off with a knife. I think they discovered that I was a girl the day I ran screaming home to tell my mother what they were doing with her cutlery.

Rabbits also featured in their commercial enterprises. The machair was alive with plump rabbits and the crofters were always complaining about the havoc being wreaked on their crops. So, together with some other young lads, my older brothers saw a window of opportunity. They went out on dark nights with a fast dog and a strong torch and in the morning young Donald went round the township with the rabbits draped over the handlebars of the bike in pairs. He sold them, on behalf of his brothers, for one shilling and sixpence per pair. The other two paid him a commission of sixpence per pair sold, but they did not know until they were adults that he had been charging the housewives sixpence per rabbit for skinning and cleaning them, thus in fact earning more than they did. He was a very good salesman and never brought one back.

My mother had a strong aversion to rabbits, dating back to her time at Oban Cottage hospital where she said that the staff had been fed nothing else. She also said that the rabbits grew fat on the corpses in Hallin cemetery and would not touch them. The rest of the family, however, could not resist the smell of rabbit meat stewing slowly in a pot with onions and a bit of turnip, and so someone had to cook them, usually me. I didn't mind the cooking, but sometimes I had to skin and clean them as well. The skinning wasn't too bad, I was quite glad when the skin came off like a glove and the carcass no longer looked like a fluffy bunny, but I had to clean them first, and the smell was just so awful that it made me feel sick. I'd rather gut ten barrels of herring than clean one rabbit. There was also a small amount of money to be made from the skins, as Willie Jordan bought them. I have no idea what happened to them next, but knowing Willie's acumen in matters of money I'm sure he had some market for them. More of him later.

One day Donald Angus came home full of excitement, as he'd been talking to some of the other boys and they had told him about two men who had asked them to round up some helpers. They were digging up a large area of the machair. One man was a doctor by the name of Kissling and the other was called Tom. My parents wondered why a German would be digging on our machair and my father said 'Polly bottles.' Donald Angus was very keen to join the digging party as the doctor was going to take them all to Askernish machair and show them how to play golf, if they worked hard. He had also mentioned teaching them to swim. They were digging for unusual things like old bones and signs of people from long ago and had no interest in the 'Polly', my brother said. My parents were a bit worried about letting him go off with strangers and made their own enquiries before giving their permission.

It transpired that the men were archaeologists and that Dr Kissling, despite his German pedigree, had long been a lover of the islands. He had lived on Eriskay for many

TO THE EDGE OF THE SEA

years and had been taking photographs and moving-pictures of the Eriskay people and their way of life. He had published his work, *Eriskay, A Poem Of Remote Lives*, and with the proceeds from it had provided a road for Eriskay. It also came out that he was so anti-Nazi that when Hitler came to power he had sent men to London to bring the doctor back to Germany for questioning. Dr Kissling had evaded capture by throwing his coat over their heads and running away. Someone also said that his brothers had been shot for conspiring to kill Hitler. True or not, he sounded pretty trustworthy, so Donald Angus was given permission to join the diggers.

Each day my brother would take some food and go down to the machair with my mother's words, 'Don't go near the sea', as a constant warning. The currents round the island are very treacherous and have taken many lives over the years. The islanders know this and respect the sea. My brother wasn't too happy about it as the doctor liked nothing better than to cool off in the sea after a hard day's digging and could not understand the reluctance of his helpers to accept swimming lessons. However, Donald Angus was allowed to take advantage of the golf lessons but did not see much point in the game and soon abandoned it.

The digging went well and they uncovered what at first they thought was a 'beehive' dwelling, but as the work proceeded they found that it was a 'wheelhouse', the updated version of the 'Atlantic roundhouse' or 'Beehive'. There were conflicting thoughts on its age but the date AD 2 was mentioned. It amazed the boys that people had lived in Kilpheder so long ago. At school they had learned that the islands had once belonged to Norway before they had been passed on to the clans as uncontrollable, but this find came from a past so distant

95

that its place in time was difficult for the young helpers to grasp. They just knew that this little dwelling-place was very, very old. Also uncovered were traces of fire and some bone-needle type artifacts and pieces of a type of slate which is found only on one of the offshore group of islands, I think it was the Monachs, so the inhabitants must have been able to travel across the sea.

We all went down as a family to see the newly uncovered *Tigh Talabhanta* (earth dwelling), as we called it, and we were surprised to see that the walls were so low. There were four chambers enclosed by four-foot-high walls connected to each other by passages, the whole encircling a larger area, probably a communal fireplace or meeting place which formed the hub of the wheel. The door apertures were also very low, three feet high at most, so we concluded that the inhabitants must have been very small people, or that this was just the base of the structure and that there had been other elevated sections of wall which had not survived. The archaeologists disagreed with our theory and we were left to wonder just who these tiny people had been and what their lives had been like living in their little communes by the sea. As we walked home we trod a little bit more carefully on the machair soil and speculated on the possibility that more civilisations from prehistoric times lay beneath it.

We could have been right as this year, a few months ago in fact, student archaeologists from English and Welsh universities found another site under the sand right on the shoreline of Kilpheder machair. It was a grave with a female skeleton, and although no news of its origin has yet reached the island it is believed, from the traces of rust in the tunnels round the burial place, to be Iron Age or later, poor little Iron Maiden, lying diagonally across her rectangular grave with a large round stone clasped in her hands, I wonder what her life was like, or who, in future centuries, will uncover our graves and speculate about our civilisation.

The excitement of the digging died down as the artifacts were taken away for testing and the team left the island. Both my older brothers were coming up for their Junior Leaving Certificate examination, so career choices were high on the agenda and neither of them wanted to conform. The traditional path for the pupils who passed the exam was to follow the *Air Falbh* (going away) path and continue their education on the mainland, eventually becoming teachers, doctors, or nurses. Other professional paths were just beginning to appear, but were viewed as 'not quite the thing' by island parents with their sights set on their children becoming members of the professions which then represented the elite of the island. So the question was: 'Are you going to be a teacher, doctor, nurse or priest or are you going to sea?' These were the only choices open to us then, long before the advent of the social studies degree.

Priests and nuns had to have vocations, and most of the candidates were said to have manifested some sign of their calling since childhood. They left for the seminaries and convents in their early teens. One of Kilpheder's most celebrated priests was Father John Morrison. During his ministry on the island he came close to thwarting the Ministry of Defence's annexing of Eochdar machair for their Guided Weapons Range. He managed to win substantial concessions for the local crofters before the might of the Army defeated him. Father John had discovered his vocation in early childhood. He was a contemporary of my mother's, and she used to tell us how his father complained bitterly about his 'useless son'. During the haymaking season John would go missing and be found behind a haystack, praying for the poor people who had no hay or corn. His father would haul him to his feet, give him a shake and tell him that prayers would not fill the stackyard. Despite all the opposition John persuaded his father that his life would be worthless unless he became a priest, and eventually permission was given. I have never known anyone more contented in their chosen field of work. Whether conducting his services or comforting the bereaved, talking to young people in their own language or fighting the islanders' corner he was the right man in the right place.

There were many priests like him who had found their niche and gloried in it. Nuns too who from childhood had wanted no other life. However there were also some little boys and girls sent off to seminaries far from their homes and committed to a life of celibacy and isolation, long before they knew whether they were 'Arthur or Martha'. Some just went along with it because they didn't want to bring shame on their families by leaving and 'causing talk'. I have never believed that wanting to have a priest in the family or 'giving a child back to God' was either humane or logical. The decision should be left until the person is old enough fully to understand the committment. How can you know at an early age that you are doing the right thing unless you are very sure that God's call comes from your heart and not from your mother? I think that old Mr Morrison did the right thing, delaying Father John's decision until it became inevitable.

In our family the question never arose. It was pretty obvious that none of us were suited to a life in the cloth, and so, 'Are you going to be a teacher, doctor, or nurse or are you going to sea?'. In my case I had no doubts. I was going to that nice place where nuns taught you to be teachers and you had lots of girls of your own age writing in your little red book, asking you to pray for them. Case closed. The boys were a bit more complicated. Donald Angus wanted to be a sailor, but not an ordinary sailor. He wanted to be a naval officer. Donald John wanted to be a policeman, but not an ordinary policeman, he wanted to be a detective and solve crimes by using his powers of deduction. I think he had just discovered Sherlock Holmes in the school library.

There was much discussion, and the results were that Donald Angus was enrolled for the Apprentice Navigation Officer's course at the Royal Technical College in Glasgow and Donald John agreed that completing his education in Fort William would be no hindrance to his ambitions. As it happens he did become a detective and attained the rank of Detective Inspector, Special Branch, at Scotland Yard, spending much of his time in the Diplomatic Protection Unit, where he rubbed shoulders with Prime Ministers and Royalty. He died young and left a huge gap in all our lives; but I think that during his too-short lifetime he had managed to achieve many of his ambitions, including solving crimes by using his powers of deduction. Returning to live in Uist was his eventual goal, as is illustrated in his song 'Uibhist nam Beanntan' (Uist of Bens), but that was not to be.

Getting two boys ready for their lives as mainland students meant that many new clothes had to be bought and this was a bit of a headache for my mother. She got most of our clothes from catalogues, but the delay between ordering and delivery was a nuisance and it was frustrating when the clothes did not fit. Fortunately there was also a local supplier called Willie Jordan. An unforgettable person and one of my favourite characters of all time.

A legend in his lifetime and beyond, Willie made an impact on all who met him and even now, when his name is mentioned in Uist, it is with affection and regret that such a larger-than-life personality is no longer around. An Irish packman, he came to our village as a comparatively young man, took up lodgings with a local family, and plied his trade there all his life till he died of old age. In his adopted family he was absolute ruler. Nobody dared to sit in Willie's chair. If you went in while he was eating you addressed no words to him. 'Sure if God meant you to eat and talk at the same time she'd have given you two mouths.' He always spoke in a mixture of Irish and Scottish Gaelic, supplemented by bits of English and confused his genders something awful.

The room which was his bedroom, shop and store was a veritable Aladdin's cave of garments wrapped in oilskin-covered bundles, and he always managed to unwrap a good three-quarters of them, searching for the goods you wanted. Human nature being what it is you bought twice as much as you intended.

During the day he'd fill his little Austin with as many packs as it would hold, and driving mostly in second gear he would do his rounds, selling locknit knickers with elasticated legs and long johns to the *bodachs* (old men) and *cailleachs* (old women) in remote areas and picking up much local gossip as he went. In the evenings he was available for business in his room where he passed on the day's news as he took your money, if you had it, and arranged payment on instalments, based solely on trust, if you were short.

Willie made a good living from the packs, but it was

not through his commercial expertise that his name still lives on in South Uist. No, this fame came from his extravagant stories and his strange bursts of drinking. Any Irishman can spin a yarn, but Willie's had a flavour of their own. Totally improbable stories delivered in his own inimitable pidgin Highland Irish. His face was large and red and once described by a visitor as 'A cross between Alfred Hitchcock and a badly finished Toby jug'. I don't know if the visitor's words were his own but they surely fitted Willie. He really enjoyed telling whoppers. His eyes would twinkle and the punch line was reached through a series of wheezy chuckles. Some of the older people he visited swallowed his tall stories hook, line and sinker, and as some of them had never gone very far from home they took Willie's version of life in Ireland as gospel. My father's ambition was to catch him out and have the last word, but Willie always managed to stay one step ahead, most of the time.

One day my father was cutting peat in a part of our croft some distance from the house and my little brother and I were taking a flask of tea out to him. As we walked along the road Willie's car came up behind us and he stopped to offer us a lift. When he heard where we were going he left his car by the side of the road and walked with us, out to the peat bog to have a word with his friend and adversary.

'That's a good spade you've got there, man.'
'Aye, Willie it'll do.'
'Begorrah but you should see the one my father had, seven times the size of that one.'
'Aye, Willie?'
'My ould man she was very big, eight feet tall and as strong as ten bulls.'
My father continued to cut the turf. Rhythmically

skimming off the grassy tussocks in squares and laying them on the bank upside down in a neat patio to receive the wet peat. He knew that another tale of Irish valour was forthcoming, and his role was merely that of an admiring audience. My brother and I knew that something good was about to happen.

'Sure and it's a warm job you're doing there, so it is. It reminds me of one day I was out with the packs in the ould country. Bejasus it was hot. I was sweating so much I was walking in puddles.'

'Aye, Willie.'

'I was walking along sweating fit to disappear when I came to a river. I set the packs down and took off every last stitch of my clothes, even my semmit. Then pure and naked as the day I was born I jumped into the river. As I hit the water steam clouded my sight and the splashes made blisters rise up on the skin on my face. I swam at sixty miles an hour to get away from the hissing of the water and after swimming for two miles or maybe ten I felt my blood come off the boil. Best get back to the packs in case the tinkers come and take them, I thought. So, round I turned and there coming towards me with her eyes flashing like bicycle lamps and his great jaws wide open was the ugliest shark I ever saw . . .'

'Sharks in Ireland? In a river? Willie?'

'Damn you, man, I said the ould country, what I did not say was that it was my ould country. Now, where was I? . . . The ugly ould devil was coming straight for me with her mouth watering and I could see that this was no time for reasoning with him. So I thrust my hand in my pocket and took out my tobacco knife . . .'

'But you were naked, Willie.'

'Saints blast you, man, I come here to pass the time of day with you and all you do is argue with me!' Willie stamped off to his car and took off with much crashing of gears. My father chuckled contentedly as he finished his cutting and drank his tea.

'You got him! You got him!' we shouted. 'Aye,' replied my father, 'till next time.'

Months of hard work selling his stuff and counting his money, and then out of the blue Willie would change his routine completely and embark on the biggest binges the island has ever known.

Taking hundreds of pounds from his money box he'd spend weeks drinking with all and sundry, treating everyone he met to bottles of the stuff. He would walk into the bar and take over. Everyone was his friend and the drinks kept coming until even the hardest headed could take no more and the the barman advised them to leave. Then a bulging Austin full of drunks and carryouts would weave its way to the bar at the other end of the island, in and out of ditches, to repeat the process there.

Sometimes the entire contingent would keep going for the duration of the binge, but mostly it was a kind of relay. Some crawled home after a day or two to be replaced by others. Willie himself was never seen to fall down or sleep, and although the driving was erratic there were never any casualties. He just kept drinking, singing, telling his dreadful stories, laughing his wheezy laugh, spending money and driving his little car backwards and forwards from bar to ditch to bar till he'd had enough. Then as suddenly as it had started it was over. Back home for twenty-four hours' sleep and back to normal again, sober as a judge for ages, or, as Willie himself would say, 'For two years or maybe ten.'

Eventually the boys were kitted out and they were off. Donald Angus left at the start of the summer holidays, as his course was about to begin. Donald John had a few more weeks at home and then he went on to Fort William. With my own Leaving Certificate exams looming at the end of the school year, tests which I did not intend to fail, I got my head down and wrestled with simultaneous equations and Latin vocabulary.

Chapter Nine

Mo *thruagh mi 'smar tha mi'n diugh*
Sadness fills my heart today

Mo *thruaigh mi 's gur muladach*
My heart is sad and sorrowful

S'e 'n gaol a thug mi'n ghille dubh
The love I gave the dark-eyed boy

A rinn an diugh mo leònadh
Today has left me mourning

WE ALL REMEMBER WHERE we were and what we were doing on the day we heard some catastrophic news. Time stood still in the little croft house on September 25th, 1952. I will never forget the song my father sang softly to himself as he prepared to leave for Wallasey hospital, where my brother Donald Angus had been taken for the amputation of his left hand. He had completed the first module of his course at the Royal Technical College and was embarking on the preliminary practical section on board his first ship, the *Kelvinbank*, sailing out of

Liverpool. The accident happened as they were docking at Birkenhead, when a rope he was handling wrapped itself round his hand with tragic results. The rope was attached to a fender, the cushion-like device used on docking ships, to avoid collision damage if the side of the vessel scraped against the structure of the dock. The *Kelvinbank* nudged the pier, the fender did its job, the swell caused the vessel to heave upwards and the rope suddenly played out, taking with it most of my brother's hand and all of his hopes of a career as a naval officer, a few weeks before his seventeenth birthday.

Each of us reacted in different ways to the message that the priest had brought us early that morning. My father, never one to hide his feelings, went outside and stood in Letty's empty stall in the byre thumping the wall and sobbing with great wracking tremors of grief coursing through his body as he railed against the God who had allowed this terrible thing to happen to his boy. Now and then he'd shout: 'Why did I listen to him?' 'Why did I let him go away?' 'He'd have been safe here.' There had been a time when my father had hoped that his eldest son would stay on the croft and work alongside him in the traditional manner, but sensing that Donald Angus had other ambitions he had not put any pressure on him. It was quite frightening for the rest of us to see our normally stable father behaving in this fashion. Shouts of laughter, we'd grown up with, shouts of anger too, when things displeased him, but these great shouts of grief shocked us all. Young Donald took the dog down to *Tobht' ic 'ille Chriosda* (Gilchrist's Ruin), the knoll where we used to search for honey in the hayfield, and he sat there with the dog by his side, like two statues staring down towards the machair for most of the day. My mother started to iron shirts, not the usual early morning

106

CROFTER'S CHILD AND BARRA COUSIN
' ... much taller than I was, fair haired and very pretty.
As if that wasn't enough, she had a kilt.'

TWINS AT BARRA SCHOOL
Mary Flora, fourth from right, middle row.
Alick Iain, first on left front row.

My Parents' Wedding Day
'... and so my father, the only son-in-law, an incomer from Benbecula,
became a South Uist crofter.'

CONVENT GIRLS
'we were 'Let Out' on Saturday and Sunday afternoons.'

THE BEN NEVIS HIKE
' ...we hiked up twice and it nearly finished me off.'

DALIBURGH ACADEMIC SCHOOL
' The old corrugated iron building by the loch.'
(Now derelict)

FORT WILLIAM SCHOOL
' ... on this site generations of children had been educated since the 18th century.'

THATCHING THE CROFT HOUSE
' ... it belongs to Donald MacDonald, a quiet dignified bard.'

CROFT HOUSE BENCH
' ... the whole of the front wall was taken up by the bench... '
(Photo by kind permission, Uist Museum.)

KYLES FLODDA SCHOOLHOUSE
'A large house with high ceilings.'

A FIELD OF STOOKS
' ... propped them up into stooks, which were gathered together to form small stacks.'

My Mother Stacking Hay
' ... when the stack yard was full there was a great feeling of security.'

task when cows were waiting to be milked. She had her back to me and I could hear sizzling noises as her tears hit the flat iron, but she herself made no sound apart from an occasional whisper of '*Meudail bheag*' (My little darling) as she slowly walked over to the other side of the kitchen to replace the cold iron with the one heating up on the stove.

The little twins, over from Barra on what was to be their final visit before coming back home, were too young to realise the enormity of it all and were discussing the drawbacks of losing a hand. There was speculation about not being able to carry presents in a suitcase. I think they were frightened by their first glimpse of parents unable to contain their heartbreak and were drawing comfort from the sound of each other's voices. I kept seeing a vision of my brother's young hands, crossed to receive the strap for defiance at school. A photograph of him, tall and proud in his college blazer, stood on the piano. Never again would I see his left hand flying over the keyboard as he tried to outplay my mother's nimble fingers. I remember feeling astonished that birds were singing outside and that people on the neighbouring croft were going about their usual chores as if nothing had happened, while in my chest a great knot of tears built up waiting for the time when it could be released. Not a day to remember too often, although it will never go away. Donald John was at Fort William school and had to cope with the news of his brother's accident alone. I'm sure he wanted to be at home with his family, although none of us could have given him much comfort.

Tragedy always leaves its mark, and my parents took many years to get over their sorrow, Donald Angus insists to this day that although it has been an inconvenience at times, the loss of his hand has not had any adverse effect on his life. He has had the pleasure of seeing his son join the Navy and have a good career as a pilot with the Fleet Air Arm, another dark-eyed boy who wore his uniform with pride. Watching the heads turn as my now silver-haired brother entered a London gathering recently, crossing the floor to greet his party with the confident stride so reminiscent of my father's walk, the thought crossed my mind that losing his hand had indeed not had much of an adverse effect on his life.

Our good friends and neighbours rallied round and as life must go on, things eventually returned to normal in the family. Donald Angus did not return to the croft but wisely embarked on rehabilitation and training to help him cope with his changed circumstances, away from the sympathy and curiosity of the islanders, which though well-meant would have served him no useful purpose.

Donald John was doing well in Fort William, writing home regularly and enclosing the occasional funny poem in his letters, mostly irreverent descriptions of the teachers whom I would meet when my turn came. My father had become even more involved with the seaweed factory, or Alginate Industries as it was now called, and young Donald with the help of his friend the dog had taken on many of the crofting chores before and after school.

The dog who had been Donald's companion in grief was typical of the dogs found on any Hebridean croft. A Border Collie type, so easy to train and intensely loyal. We had a succession of them over the years, and although we had the odd Labrador and Spaniel as well, none could match the Collie Cross as an extra source of help on the croft. They seemed to have an in-built sense of time and knew just which chore came next.

Our neighbour John had a dog which was quite remarkable. John's cows did their summer grazing in a field which was separated from the main part of his croft by a distance of a mile or so across two main roads, and he would walk out there, with the dog, twice daily for the milking. When the autumn set in and the grazing was getting poor, he would bring them home for the evening milking and keep them in the byre overnight with full mangers to supplement their feed. Then he would walk them back out to the field again in the morning.

One day when they had reached the field his dog jumped up, and with his nose he lifted the latch on the field-gate, causing it to swing open. As John stood by, the dog herded the cows on to the road and headed them homewards along the main road. When a car approached, the dog ran alongside the cows, and by barking and nipping at their heels he nagged them into an orderly file by the roadside, keeping them there until the vehicle had passed, and all John had to do was walk behind his herd. When they arrived at the main croft the dog repeated the unlatching process with the gate in front of the byre, and peeling the cows off one by one he sent them into the byre to find their stalls. Cows like their own stalls and their own manger so in they went and stood waiting for John to come and milk them.

This went on for a few weeks, and as John was a creature of habit he and his dog would walk past our house each evening at about five o'clock. Sometimes John would stop for a chat, usually about the dog, while it got on with taking the cows on homewards and into the byre as usual. Then one afternoon John wrenched his ankle badly and was hobbling around the house, dreading the long walk out to the grazing field in the evening. He kept putting it off and putting it off until he could no longer do so, and getting a jacket and a stick, hobbled outside and called the dog. He called and called but no dog came. As John cursed and fumed and hobbled about looking for his faithless hound he happened to look out towards the grazing field. There in the distance he could see a long line of brown cows plodding towards Kilpheder cross-roads, being chivvied along by a busy black and white dog. His cows and his dog. From that day on John let the dog do the evening run by itself, and on the dot of five o'clock each evening we would see him loping past our croft on his way out to the grazing field to bring John's cows home for milking.

As the years went by the dog and John, a bachelor who lived alone, kept each other company and worked the croft together. John was a diabetic, and from time to time had to go into the local hospital for treatment. When this happened the dog would sit outside the hospital, under the window of the men's ward, and stay there until John was discharged. The treatment often took days, but the dog stayed there day and night, refusing any efforts to feed it or move it until his master was ready to go home.

Our local hospital in those days was known as The Sacred Heart Hospital, staffed largely by a band of Sacred Heart nuns, and a much smaller building than the present large, well-equipped Daliburgh Hospital which has grown around it, as new wings have been added. It was originally called Bute Hospital and was given to the islanders by the Marchioness of Bute in 1894, when it was staffed by three women. That is the recorded account of its origin, but my auntie Christina's version told to me during my post-pneumonia days was a little bit different. I stress that this is mere hearsay and apologise in advance to surviving family members of the good Marchioness without whose generosity many of my ancestors would have been denied medical care.

Auntie's story had it that the islanders had asked many rich people for help in their struggle against illness and disease but no interest had been shown. Eventually the Marchioness of Bute told them to start building and that she would pay for all the materials if they managed to have the hospital built and roofed in a stated period of time. I forget the exact number of days, but according to auntie it was a very precise time, from sun-up on a specific date till sun-down on another, some time later. Now the period of time she had chosen was one where for many years previously, without fail, the weather had been appalling. Gales and lashing rain had prevented outdoor work and the proposed site for the hospital had been reduced to a quagmire. In other words the Marchioness had set the islanders an impossible task. However, as auntie said, 'That year God was on their side. He sent the wind and rain to Bute and sent Uist a hard frost instead.' The builders worked day and night and the roof was in place on the day which the Marchioness had stipulated. She passed the money over and the island got its hospital.

Like the Nunton Convent story, I don't know how much of island folklore is based on fact, but auntie had such a profound dislike of all landlords and so-called benefactors that it may have distorted her memory. According to her, MacDonald of Boisdale was so corrupt that eventually his body decomposed while he was still alive and he died screaming in agony. There was also a story about a Ferguson who lived in the big house in South Lochboisdale and who cheated the crofters so badly that on the night he died many people saw his evil soul being taken up into the sky in a black, flame-encircled chariot, driven by the devil himself. A very bloodthirsty little person, my auntie.

The house was very quiet when the two older brothers had left. Alick came over from Barra as the aunties were finding that looking after two children, however well behaved, was a bit too much for them; but Mary Flora stayed with them until the end of the school year. My parents were thinking of joining in the current trend of having a new house built and were always looking at plans and discussing sites. I could not imagine any home other than our little thatched house, but I thought that it would be nice to have running water and electricity and a roof which I could trust. The previous winter we had woken up in the middle of the night to find that the fierce wind which had gusted to gale force during the night had blown a large amount of thatch off the roof directly above the bedroom, and we could see the stars through the rafters. It was a frightening experience and one which has left me with a fear of night storms. Each crofter who wanted to replace his old house was given a loan to finance labour and materials, and if the building conformed to the required standards and specifications he would then be given a grant which was deducted from the loan. There were only two types of house plans available at that time – a long rectangular single-storey type and the more conventional square bungalow with a bit sticking out at the front. They both had three bed-rooms, a living room, a large kitchen and a bathroom.

By now we had graduated from sand on the floor to a square of linoleum, but otherwise the house had changed little over the years. The main bedroom still had an assortment of beds and our only wardrobe, with a full-length mirror set into the door. The *trannsa* (passage) which led to the kitchen had a tongued-and-grooved wall holding stout coat hooks groaning with outdoor coats and jackets. The kitchen, which was also the living-room and dining-room, still looked the same as it had done on the night my mother had dropped the dumpling. A square room, lit by two small deep windows during the day, and by a Tilley lamp suspended from the ceiling at night. Against the back wall was a large built-in dresser. The piano stood next to it, and a small table covered with song-books was tucked into a corner by the closet door. A table and four chairs stood against the inner wall with four more folding chairs (army surplus) leaning against the bit of wall that was left. Opposite the table was the black stove with a high mantelpiece above it. A large pot full of bubbling water and a steaming kettle always stood on the stove. The mantel shelf was adorned with two brass candlesticks and some framed photos of relatives standing in stiff poses. A string, permanently full of drying socks or tea towels, was slung under it. Above the mantel hung a picture of the Pope with his hand raised in blessing. Shelves to one side of the stove held cooking pots and other odds and ends and on the other side was a large box full of peat. To the side of the stove, in front of the dresser was the *seuthar mór* (big chair), a Rexine-covered high-backed armchair. By the door stood a box-like structure supporting the water buckets, and next to that the whole length of the front wall was taken up by the bench which had only changed in that it now also had a covering of linoleum, which made it even less comfortable.

Last summer the twins and I sat in a similar house, one of the few left on the island still used as a home and not a holiday 'let'. It belongs to Donald MacDonald, a quiet dignified bard who lives in South Lochboisdale. We all knew each other years ago and we spent a very pleasant hour sitting on the bench by his stove, with its peat fire, talking about old times and marvelling at how large island families had managed to fit into such a small room. As Donald said, 'We were always on the move, young and old, doing something on the croft, and when it got dark and the grown-ups sat down, the children went to bed.' Although he still lives in his lovely little thatched house Donald has evidently moved with the times. When we were leaving he introduced the speckled hens who came up to inspect us as The Spice Girls.

My parents had decided on the shape of their new house and had chosen the site. Negotiations were going ahead with one of the local builders. Unlike the present day 'kit houses' which are springing up all over the island, the new croft-houses of my father's time were built on site in the traditional way. It was boom time for anyone who knew how to build a house, and even a few who couldn't build a decent peat stack had jumped on the band-wagon. One new house in our village was condemned as being a hazard to its inhabitants within a couple of years of being erected. Still, we were fortunate with ours, as it is still in use over forty years later.

At school we soldiered on doing mock exams and generally getting ready for the big one at the end of the year. Our music teacher decided to try and involve the adult members of the community in a Gilbert and Sullivan production, but gave up, as the Hebridean accent made it sound so strange that he couldn't bear it. Also the play on words, so typical of the operetta, went right over the cast's head. Gaelic humour, like that of the Irish and Welsh, is often sharp and caustic, unlike the gentle irony of the English tongue. His comments at school the next day were a bit unkind as he had really wanted to produce something spectacular. I don't think the audience would have been too appreciative anyway, judging by the reaction to a concert arranged by the

Scottish Co-operative Society in an effort to advertise its growing number of food stores on the islands. They enlisted the help of some local performers, like my father, and sent a woman singer and a magician as their contribution to the programme. The local artistes got the usual rapturous applause. The magician went down well, but the poor woman didn't stand a chance. She was obviously a trained opera singer well past her sell-by date, and as she screamed and trembled her way through 'Oh My Beloved Father' the normally well-mannered and appreciative Hebridean audience convulsed with laughter and some wag from the back of the hall shouted 'For God's sake send for the vet!' People still remember her though, while the name of the magician has long been forgotten.

One bit of excitement in my final year at Daliburgh happened during the dinner-hour, which we spent ambling about the school playground waiting for the bell to ring, after walking up to the Co-op to spend our pennies on sticky buns to fill the gap left by the school dinner. Someone noticed that the Swedish houses were enveloped in smoke, and the cry, 'Casimer Place is on fire!', went up. As the wind swirled the smoke around we could see that two of the houses were indeed ablaze and the smell of burning creosote drifted towards us. Fortunately there were no casualties, although the houses burned to the ground. There was only one fire engine on the island at the time, and as it was based at Benbecula airport, nearly twenty miles away, it took some time to get to the fire. All the crew could do was to spray the other houses and generally contain the blaze so that only two families lost their homes and belongings. We did very little school work that afternoon as none of us had seen a fire on that scale before. Although quite frightening it was an awesome spectacle.

When I went home that day, bursting to tell my mother all about the fire, I discovered that it was old news, as a tinker wife was sitting on the bench telling her all about it. Usually, if my mother saw tinkers approaching she would lock the door and hide. Hebridean tinkers did not have the glamour of the colourful Romany tribes. They came out of nowhere every summer and camped in their strangely shaped tents on the common ground out at Carisheval, with their ramshackle carts, skinny horses, snappy dogs and ragged children; they were not a welcome band. They were suspected of stealing peat from the bogs and generally helping themselves to anything they could find around the houses as they travelled about, selling their pails and clothes pegs, and asking for handouts of milk and eggs. They also asked for rags or old clothes. Our cast-offs were usually of the collar and waistband held-together-by-a-hole variety, and as the tinkers wore most of their collection they were a strangely dressed group. The islanders are generous people and they would always give to the tinkers, especially if they had a babe or two with them, but I think they feared them and that is why they were treated with suspicion. Tinkers, especially the women, were said to have supernatural powers and were pretty free with their curses if you didn't buy their wares. They were reputed to possess 'the evil eye', and if they looked at your beasts the wrong way they would bear dead calves or catch diseases and die.

So I was most amazed to find my mother apparently entertaining this tinker wife. She finished her cup of tea, sold my mother some clothes pegs and left after reading my mother's palm and telling her that generosity was her key to a happier life. Naturally my mother embarked on this path straight away by putting some eggs in the woman's pail and filling an old whisky bottle with milk for her. The tinker wife left, blessing us all and promising to come back again next year – words which made her hostess go pale. It transpired that my mother had been out at the end of the house trying to work out where all the smoke was coming from and had been very worried in case the school was on fire. When she came indoors the tinker wife was at the stove making herself a pot of tea. Not wishing to be cursed, especially as her children might at that moment be in a blazing building, my mother had no option but to make the lady as welcome as possible.

The school year drew to a close, and the lucky children whose parents could afford the cost went off to the annual *Comunn Na H-Oigridh* (Society of Youth) camp on the beautiful Isle of Skye. Donald John had gone once, the trip financed by the aunties as a reward for settling down and working hard at school, and he had enjoyed it immensely. On his return he had regaled us all with tales of the old castle at the head of Loch Dunvegan, the seat of the clan MacLeod. He told us tales about a *bean Shìdhe* (Fairy Woman) who had once given the clan chief a *bratach* (Cloak) and a *sionnsair Airigid* (Silver Chanter) with which the player could play any tune to perfection. Donald John had also learned to peel potatoes during that week, as he had been caught writing a poem about one of the less popular organisers. The camp was primarily a meeting place for young Gaelic speakers from all over the Islands and was very well supported each summer.

The exams were over and we were all convinced that we had really blown it and that no bursary with which we could finance our further education would be forthcoming. However, one morning when we had all but forgotten about the tests, the headmaster came in to tell us that the results were the best ever at the school and that our entire class had passed. A summer at home, and then I'd be joining Donald John at Fort William. The sadness of the previous months was gradually fading.

Chapter Ten

THE CLANGING OF A bell fitted in perfectly with my dream. I was on the boat bound for Mallaig and it was a very rough crossing. The bell got louder and louder and someone in my dream shouted 'Abandon Ship!' I leapt out of bed and climbed the rope ladder, which was in fact my cubicle curtain, shouting in Gaelic: 'Where are the lifeboats? How long have we got?' The nun in the doorway ignored the pantomime and chanted, 'Praised be the Lord Jesus Christ!' Sleepy voices answered: 'Praised for evermore, Amen.' Her footsteps moved on to the next dorm and a voice called out: 'You've got three years and the lifeboats have sunk!' My first morning at the convent had dawned.

To start the senior secondary phase of your education in the forties and fifties you had to be a good sailor. The schools were located in Inverness, Portree and Fort William, and most of the Catholics went to Fort William or Inverness while the sons of the more wealthy Catholic islanders paid to go to to the private school at Fort

Augustus Abbey. The Non-Catholics favoured Portree school which was on the largely Protestant Isle of Skye, and was thus avoided by Catholic parents when nominating preferences for their children. Neither Fort William nor the Academy School in Inverness were Catholic schools – just the usual inter-denominational mix – but that didn't seem to matter, and if you had passed the Junior Leaving Certificate examination Inverness-shire Education Authority guaranteed the payment of your living expenses at the school of your choice for three years.

The Minch lay between you and your school, whichever one you chose, and you faced six crossings a year. The journeys alone would be enough to put many people off, but we took them in our stride, as indeed we had to, they were a necessary evil, and we were so proud of having joined ranks of the chosen. As I packed all the newly name-tagged clothes into my new suitcase and prepared to go with Donald John to Fort William I was filled with excitement. The dream which had originated in the junk room at Kyles Flodda after listening to auntie's stories was about to come true.

Both parents went with us to Lochboisdale to see us off on the boat, and as the bus driver came out to help with the luggage he said, 'My Goodness, you're sending two away this year'. They both looked very proud. Naturally we travelled by boat. Planes were for tourists and more wealthy islanders and the journey was unfailingly awful. I have heard it said that many a local seaman who had sailed the Bay of Biscay without disgracing himself had cause to dread the trip between Oban or Mallaig and Lochboisdale. Something to do with tides and cross-currents, my father said; but with the enjoyable experience of travelling to South Africa by sea behind me I think it had more to do with the boats. The crossing took anything from six to twelve hours, depending on the weather, and who can depend on weather in the Hebrides, where you can have a lovely sunny day in December and a howling gale in August? Between the age of fourteen and twenty I spent a minimum of 216 hours on the water and fed the herring with monotonous regularity.

That night the boat carried a large number of potential doctors, teachers, nurses and at least one fledgling priest that I know of, students from Barra, Eriskay, Benbecula and South Uist, ranging in ages from about fifteen to eighteen. The Barra students had already crossed over from Castlebay on the *Loch Earn* and were transferring to the Mallaig boat at Lochboisdale. Some preferred the Oban route and would wait for the *Loch Earn* to make its return journey to Castlebay, then join it for the Tiree/ Oban sailing; but most of them favoured the *Loch Mor* and the Mallaig way.

Many of the older Uist students were greeting specific members of the Barra contingent with more than friendship, and after the boat sailed I was surprised to find my brother kissing a pretty young lady from Vatersay by the name of Nancy, behind a lifeboat. Fort William, and indeed this next section of my education, were beginning to look more interesting by the minute.

The boat docked at Mallaig very early in the morning, and there was quite a delay before the train left, but there was one consolation. If the boat was delayed due to bad weather the train departure would be put back for anything up to three hours, so that boat passengers could make the connection. Having deposited our belongings at the left luggage office and been given a receipt, we passed the time trying to find something to eat, and since most of us had experienced a seasick, sleepless night, we staggered around Mallaig trying to stay awake.

The train journey, along one of the most picturesque routes in the United Kingdom, was spent in a daze as the rocking motion of the old steam train made one's eyes even heavier, and every time you nodded off someone would leap up to close the windows to keep the smoke and flakes of soot out as the train passed under bridges and viaducts. At last we arrived at Fort William, the capital of Lochaber, and hauled ourselves and our bags through the town to our new homes.

The town has had its name played with over the years since the days when it was settled by the followers of troops sent in to keep the unruly seventeenth-century Highlanders in their place. The names Maryburgh, Duncansburgh and Gordonsburgh failed to survive, and the name which reminds us of the town's primary purpose is the one by which it is known today – *An Gearasdan*, or 'the Fort'.

On digging a bit more deeply into the origins of one of my favourite towns, I had the good fortune to talk to the Curator of The West Highland Museum, Fiona Marwick, earlier this year. She told me that the growth of the town could be followed by tracing its industrial pattern. The workers on various industrial projects had come to work and had stayed to settle. The influx which had begun with the military continued with the people brought to the area by Thomas Telford's Caledonian Canal, the West Highland Railway, the British Aluminium Company, Hydro Electric Power, and the Pulp and Paper Mill. There has also been a distillery there, even since before the railway. Industries may close down and workers move on but Fort William will always have the towering Ben Nevis behind it, the glittering Loch Linnhe in front of it and charming inhabitants like Miss Marwick to ensure that its year-round attraction for visitors remains. As Provost John Cameron put it so well in his 1954 address, 'Fort William is the one good turn which Cromwell did for Scotland' (*The Burgh of Fort William 1875–1975, by Walter Cameron*).

On our first bleary-eyed introduction to Fort William we were in no fit state to appreciate either its historic significance or its charms, but we were introduced to another of its features – the record rainfall figures with which the mighty Ben blesses it.

The boys in our group boarded at the boy's hostel, a fairly relaxed establishment with a nice friendly matron in charge. It was located next to the school, and from all reports was a great place to live. According to my brother, who had already spent a year there, nothing worth mentioning ever happened, and there were no tales to tell. On the other hand the girls were housed in the Convent and that's another story.

The Convent, formerly Invernevis House, was once the home of D.P. MacDonald of Invernevis Distillery, one of the original Comissioners of the Burgh, way back in 1875. In my day it was home to the Order of Notre Dame nuns and sundry female boarders. My own memories of Fort William are dominated by the Convent and events which took place there, as I had thought about it and dreamed of going there since early childhood. The building resembled a large country house, surrounded by high walls, and the gardens were immaculate green lawns bordered with roses and graceful willow trees. Coming from a treeless island where growing anything ornamental was a battle, it all looked so well-ordered and colourful.

The interior, all dark panelling and polished floors, was in two sections, as part of the house was for the

123

exclusive use of 'other' nuns. The ones who took no part in the day-to-day running of the boarding enterprise and whom we only saw in the chapel. As always, a cousin of my mother's popped up, this time among the 'other' nuns, one who had been in the Order from her teenage years and was now pretty old. Although she sent for me once and came over to the visitor's sitting room to talk to me, we could find little common ground. She spent most of the time asking me for Gaelic words which she had forgotten, and kept saying, 'You are so young to be away from your mother.' 'Amen to that', I thought. 'Try four and a half.' She gave me some stale sweets and said that she would pray for my immortal soul, and I never saw her again.

Our part of the house was pretty functional. Three floors and a little attic divided into dormitories, bathrooms, a study, recreation room, refectory, pharmacy, infirmary and a few offices. I visited the nuns some years after leaving and the impressions I left with were the smell of beeswax and incense, home-made lemonade and the most peaceful silence imaginable. I know it was holiday time and the boarders were not there, but it wasn't just that. Have you ever noticed the silence of an empty church? It has a totally different feel to that of an empty house, or any other building, It is a silence so complete that it wraps itself around you and a feeling of peace comes through. I felt that on my return visit although I had never sensed it when I lived there. Now the Convent has gone, demolished in 1965 to make way for the large Belford Hospital and only the imprint of the back gate, filled in with concrete, remains to evoke memories.

We Island girls were only part of the full complement of Convent boarders, as pupils from Mallaig, Morar,

Arisaig and other Highland areas too distant for them to be day-pupils at Fort William Senior Secondary school, also spent the school term there. They could go home at weekends if they wished, but quite often they just stayed on, preferring to spend the weekend 'out times' with their contemporaries. We all got along very well together, and I had no shortage of friends. But I suspect that having a good looking older brother at the school may have had something to do with my popularity. My cousin and friend from Barra days, now tall with long fair hair, was also there, as was the cousin from Mallaig, who was in an older group; but we all had different friends now, and although seeing them again gave my life a sense of continuity we went our separate ways. It was great living with so many girls of my own age, mixing with new people from a different background, and I spent many enjoyable weekends in Arisaig and Morar with my new acquaintances and their hospitable families.

During my boarding days I didn't see much of the gardens, which had so impressed me on arrival. We always had to use the tradesmen's entrance at the back of the building, and only once did I sit under the willows and admire the roses. That was after I had suffered a bout of mumps and was put out there to get some fresh air. Come to think of it I never saw anybody else using the garden either, apart from the old gardener and the two nuns who helped him to cut the grass and trim the bushes.

We studied in the study and ate in the refectory and lived in the dorms in our little cubicles which were furnished with a bed, a chair and a locker, with a jug and bowl on top. We were in groups of six to ten to a dorm, with a senior girl in charge. We prayed in the chapel, and we did an awful lot of that. Not even living with the aunties prepared me for the amount of attention the Almighty would require during my teenage years.

'Shivering in the grey dawn' is a much overworked phrase, but it describes exactly the condition of the girls scurrying between bathrooms and cubicles with jugs of lukewarm water for the morning wash before dressing in our navy-blue uniforms. Beds were made, hospital style – at least that's what they called it – but I can't remember seeing too many beds with a flat pleated counterpane folded into a knife-edge crease along the edge of the bed and drawn into perfect matching triangles at each corner, in any hospital. Our dormitories were inspected after the beds were made and before we lined up for chapel just before seven o'clock in the morning, unless it was a Saturday when we had a 'lie-in' until seven-thirty. The combined effects of running around like a demented housewife and kneeling upright for three-quarters of an hour speaking Latin before breakfast made me faint frequently, and in the end I was excused morning Mass except on Sundays and Holidays of Obligation. This happened only in my second year, and it surprises me how many times your head can hit a wooden floor and remain intact.

Breakfast was very frugal, as indeed were all the meals – just above starvation level – or at least that's what it seemed like to an island child brought up on the bounty of land and sea, and they appeared to be a month apart. After breakfast we all had household duties to perform. They were real sweeping, scrubbing, polishing, dish-washing duties, which left me thinking longingly of bed time till I got used to it, and, as we plodded off to school through the teeming Lochaber rain the day already seemed a week old.

The school which we attended was the old Fort William Senior Secondary. On this site generations of children had been educated since the eighteenth century, and there is a present-day primary school carrying on the tradition. However, in 1960 the secondary pupils were moved out of the Burgh across the river Lochy to the newly-built Lochaber High School, a large modern school better equipped to deal with the escalation in numbers brought about by the increase in population and the statutory raising of the school-leaving age.

From the Convent on the Lochy side of the town we walked past the Alexandra hotel, through the Parade which was once a military parade-ground, and along the main street, pausing to admire the window display of tartan skirts and vegetable dyed woollens in a shop called *Mairi Nic an T-Saoir* (Mary MacIntyre). The items on display were not priced, but we knew well that if we needed to ask the price we couldn't afford the goods, so we contented ourselves by dreaming a little before walking on past the Italian ice-cream cafe, the Town Hall, and on to the far end of the town where the school stood next to the Boys' Hostel and just past The West End Hotel.

The front windows of most classrooms looked out over Loch Linnhe towards the white houses of Caol and the art students were often taken across the road to a shelter on the lochside where they sketched the loch in all its moods. Sometimes the teacher would have to evict a poor demented local woman whom we cruelly called 'Daft Sarah', who spent a lot of time round the shelter occasionally enlivening our lessons by lifting her skirts and 'mooning' in the direction of the school windows from across the road.

The school offered a wide range of well taught subjects, and the faculty, led by an eccentric but kindly headmaster, had the usual mixture of characters. Gaelic was superbly taught in great depth by a Mr MacKinnon from Skye. I often wondered if he was related to my landlady in Robson street, but could not summon up the courage to ask. In those days familiarity had no part in your dealings with teachers. Mr Murphy was our inspirational and fiery-tempered English teacher. There was always a rush to grab a back seat when you entered his classroom. We all knew that if someone at the back offended him, he would spare himself the walk to the back of the class and slap someone at the front instead. Our art teacher was a lady who was rumoured to have obscure health problems and often arrived at school with bruises on various parts of her body, having fallen off her scooter. I have reason to remember her, as I failed the history part of my Higher Art examination because she had given the only other candidate and myself the wrong book-list to study. When exam time came I was word perfect on the lives of artists whom nobody wanted to know about. The teacher only discovered her error after the exams were over and was almost suicidal in her remorse; so we ended up comforting her. As it didn't blight my life in any way I forgave her a long time ago. School lunches were served in the Garrison Canteen, a short distance away, and walking there and back took care of most of our mid-day break; so only at the end of the school day did we go back to the Convent.

Nuns at that time, not the trendy liberated sisters of the present day, were quite an intimidating sight at close quarters. The nuns at our convent wore it all. Black hooded cloaks and stiff white wimples with faces and fingers attached, and rosary beads and bunches of keys rattled as they rustled and creaked along the highly polished wooden floors of the corridors. All except Sister

Rachael, who 'kerlumphed' along, as some of her toes had been amputated, and we really appreciated this early warning system.

At first glance the faces looked kindly and pious, but with some of them this was mere window-dressing. For instance, the one known to the girls as 'Baby Grace' was pious but definitely not kind. She was a cherubic little dumpling of a nun, and even in her austere habit looked cute and cuddly, but she took the most sadistic pleasure in humiliating girls in front of an audience, and would not have failed selection tests for the Gestapo. We all feared and hated her, and I'm sure she killed many a potential vocation stone dead.

Sister Rachel was in charge of our welfare in all departments during my first year and was a mixture of tolerance and bad temper. She was replaced by another nun, Paul Mary, and we all agreed that it was a change for the better. Although she could be as mean as a glove full of scorpions when crossed, she could be manipulated and was a real soft touch for a sob story. I had reason to be thankful for this, and remember her with great affection – but more of that later. A converted Anglican, she genuinely tried to understand and uphold the rules of her adopted faith. She had an almost pathological hatred of make-up, and we girls were her cross to bear; however, she was determined to mould us into nice young Catholic ladies despite our efforts to the contrary.

Then there was an Irish nun, Sister Rose, who was so immersed in her devotion that she was already halfway to heaven and gave little indication of inhabiting the same planet as the rest of us. Her duties included supervising our meals which she did in the most absent-minded manner. One morning at breakfast a girl swallowed a mouthful of scalding tea and burned herself. She rushed up to the rostrum where Rose was immersed in some liturgical tome and gasped, 'Please, Sister, I've burnt my throat!' Sister Rose raised her eyes from her book and whispered, 'Hush, child, offer your pain to the Lord and rub the burn with soap.' She should have joined an enclosed order where her love affair with her maker would not have to be interrupted so often by his more tiresome creations.

If I were to be asked which features of the Convent mattered most to me, I would answer the nuns, because they were all over the place, and the post-table, because it kept us going. All our mail was laid out there in the morning after breakfast, and, as you can imagine, letters were precious links with home. My parents were very good letter-writers and wrote every week without fail. One would write to my brother and the other to me, and we exchanged the letters at school. The aunties also wrote and sent the odd ten-bob note now and then, but my father's letters were the ones we both enjoyed the most, as he saved up little nuggets of island life and his own day-to-day activities to amuse us:

> We had a great time yesterday at the sheep dipping. I know you are thinking that I have never said that before and you are right! I hate the stink of the dip and I always get the rotten job of catching the sheep as they come through the trough. At least three times out of ten they knock me over and I end up lying on the ground with a wet sheep running over my face. Yesterday was good though. Some of John's flock had gone missing and as there were more than enough men at the fank to send our sheep through, we left them there and went looking for the lost ewes. You know that John's dog is cleverer than anything in Kilpheder with half the number of

legs so we let him do the tracking. We followed him along the way towards South Lochboisdale and over the back of the hill to Glendale and there they were, on their holidays.

We had never been to Glendale before and it is a great place. I had seen it from the sea at the time of the 'Polly', but only the lights as it was night time and we were always in a hurry. It is stuck away behind the hill and as there is no road the people have to carry all their food and anything else they need from the shops, over the hill, in sacks, on their backs. John was saying that they must be quite wild and different to the rest of us, living like that so isolated and lonely, but when one of them came out and called us in for a bite to eat he was willing enough to follow me into the house while the dog kept an eye on the sheep.

It was a stone-built house, a lot better than mine or John's, with a slate roof and skylights for the upstairs and a garden outside full of flowers which we could never grow here as they get the sun but not the wind. The old man and his wife were very pleasant and quite refined and they sat us down to a table all set up with a cloth and all the trimmings with a great variety of food in nice dishes. When we were leaving I thanked them and John added his bit, '*Chaidh sibh gu móran dragh, cha ruigeadh sibh a leas, tha sinne cho amh ribh fhéin.*' (You needn't have gone to so much trouble, we are just as uncivilised as yourselves). He'd have done better to have let his dog do the talking . . .

Letters, parcels, and of course seeing my brother at school every day, soon took care of homesickness, but we all counted the days until the holidays. So we settled down to our new way of life – a busy one – and although the Convent regime was rather harsh the strict rules gave us a feeling of security; but as with all young people, we were not too appreciative of that point at the time.

Chapter Eleven

IN MY CHILDHOOD DAYS bath night meant the old strip-wash routine. You went into the little room called the closet with an enamel basin or the tin bath full of warm water from the kettle and a bar of Lifebuoy soap. You stripped and sponged and washed and soaped yourself clean as far as the limited facilities and lack of privacy allowed. At Mistress MacKinnon's Glasgow residence there had been a bath in what she called the water closet, but the bath, a strange pear-shaped container on four clawed legs was always full of folded sheets, so we didn't use it. So the first time that I was totally immersed in warm soapy water, at the Convent, was one of the most wonderful experiences of my life. It eclipses childbirth, seeing Table Mountain wrapped in its tablecloth in a pink dawn and even the colours of a Vermont Fall.

Baths in the Convent, like everything else, were timetabled and timed. I still remember my place on the list. It was 6.45 p.m. till 7.15 p.m. every Wednesday. As the temperature was always pretty low around the building, bath times were the only times when I felt really warm. I have never forgotten the feeling of comfort and security I experienced when having that first bath. At various stages in my life when things have been been stressful and frayed around the edges, my first instinct is to head for the bath.

Naturally, a first time for anything is full of pitfalls, and the bath was no exception. Never would I admit to anyone else that it was my first time. A certain amount of heart searching wasted some of the precious half hour as I stood there naked trying to work out whether I should jump in or insinuate myself gradually under the water. Having decided on the latter I got in and found that I seemed to have over-filled the bath. It was a very large one and I was a bit of a shrimp. So I half sat, half floated around and tried sticking my big toe into the tap for safety, but that didn't work and I went under a few times. Eventually I found that the overflow slit provided a good toehold and the rest of the time was bliss. As the great unwashed became the squeaky clean, I was hooked on mod. cons. forever.

On my return to the study I still felt a warm glow, and as I wrestled with the translation of 'Quae cum Hannibal . . .' I had the greatest difficulty concentrating. My eyes were heavy and I was almost asleep. Suddenly a cross voice in my ear hissed, 'You get up there and clean that bloody bath!' . . . Alas nobody had prepared me for the etiquette of bathroom hygiene. I thought the bath cleaned itself as it emptied and had left it to do so. 'You can take the girl out of the heather, but you can't take the heather out of the girl.' To say that I was mortified is putting it mildly. A mainland dweller, the girl who berated me had no doubt been having baths from infancy and had no idea of my ignorance. She made darned sure that everyone in the study knew of my filthy habits and general lack of couth. I could have died of shame. To this day when visitors arrive unexpectly, my first thought is, 'Help! Is the bathroom clean?'

Sister Magdalene had shown me how to clean forks with a strange grey powder and had also given me some driving lessons on the 'bumper'. This was a heavy square pad with a very long wooden handle with which I had to polish the corridor every day. I have painful recollections of that handle embedding itself in my stomach on its return journey the first time I used it. I do wish that somebody had shown me how to clean a bath. It would have been a better preparation for real life and would have spared me much misery.

Happily there was always something new happening to divert us, and so my notoriety soon died down. One week the town was full of young men in shorts and running shoes, jogging along, and we admired them covertly as we stepped out of their way whilst walking to school in the morning. They were preparing for the gruelling marathon up to the top of Ben Nevis. Excitement among the locals was high and some local boys seemed to be in with a chance of winning. In fact previous years had seen Fort William being well represented in the winner's list, with the names Kearney and Campbell jostling for top honours. The marathon had started off as a purely Lochaber event with budding athletes who wanted to make their name challenging an established Ben runner to defend his honour. It had grown into a major mountain marathon with athletes, male and female, from all over the country taking part, but of course due to its origins there was always much joy when a local won. While I was at the Convent a local girl, Kathleen Connochie, gained the distinction of setting a new record.

We could not even contemplate the idea of running up Ben Nevis. We hiked up twice and it nearly finished us off. Personally I found it frustrating, as the weather was dull on both occasions, and although sitting in a cloud at the summit was a strange damp experience the view was obscured by mists. We went up in a group with the more energetic members of our class at school and as the town children no doubt had other weekend pursuits planned with their families, the group was composed almost entirely of Convent girls and Hostel boys, led by a teacher or two.

We followed the Achintee trail, and although it required no ropes or pitons, it was definitely more of a climb than a walk. The descent was hair-raising, as the boys thought it amusing to give you a push just when the effort of making the soles of your boots grip the steeply sloping trail was playing havoc with your knee-joints. As you flew down the trail, frantically clawing at thin air you tried to gain some braking control over your boots which seemed to have acquired a personality of their own. The only way to do this was by flinging your body sideways and backwards at the same time. This manoeuvre stopped you, by throwing you backwards on to the ground as you prayed that you would land on grass and not on a rock. Amusing to watch but horrible to experience. The group leaders walked in front of us ready to act as a last-ditch safety barrier, and repeatedly tried to restore order; but there wasn't much they could do. Two years ago I hiked the trail to the summit of Mount Mansfield, the highest peak in Vermont, and on the way down I caught myself looking over my shoulder waiting for a push.

As we got caught up in the hurly burly of teenage life it would have been easy to forget that Uist ever existed;

everything was so different and sometimes even my brother looked unfamiliar when I caught sight of him in the playground. Whether it was town living or merely the fact that he was growing up, he just seemed so much more self-assured. The letters from home helped to keep the link strong and we also had the occasional brief few minutes spent at the station with my father when he went to Glasgow to do recordings. He didn't spend too much time away from home, just went there, did the recording and got straight back to the island. The croft, the seaweed factory and the building of the new house kept him busy, but like my mother he never forgot to sit down once a week and write to us.

I am going to Glasgow on Saturday week to record some more stuff. Come to the station to meet the Mallaig train and we can have a few minutes together. I expect your mother will want me to bring you half the Co-op and a barrel of salt herring, so would you write to her and ask for something small and easy to carry? Remember that the train does not stop for long so don't waste any time pretending to be shy. I know I'll be wearing my Sunday clothes and looking very *Gallta* [Like a Lowlander] but it'll only be me without my dungarees. It will be great to see you both.

We are all well here. Your brothers and sister are working hard at school at least that is what they tell me. Old Mary By The Canal was over yesterday and she was asking after you both. Her old 'Bad Dog' got into trouble last week. He was suspected of worrying Neil's sheep and Neil came over to Mary's with his gun ready to do the business. He had already spoken to Mary and she had agreed that the dog had to go. When he got to her house the 'Bad Dog' had just finished a bowl of porridge and was starting on a plate of bacon and eggs with a slice of black pudding and a sausage on the side. Mary was crying her eyes out and keening, 'Cò a ris a bhruidhneas mise a nochd? Cò a bhios 'gam fheitheamh le fàilte mhór?' ('Who will I talk to tonight? Who will give me a big welcome when I come home?') It was all too much for Neil. Nearly in tears himself, he said 'Any dog who has a better breakfast than I do every day has no need to eat sheep. It must have been another dog. Just keep him tied up near the house for a few days till we catch the real killer.'

Well I have my own thoughts about the whole affair and B.D. had better not look sideways at our sheep or Mary's wiles won't save him from a lead earplug . . .

The little packages my father gave us at the station, and also the larger parcels which sometimes appeared on the post-table, had one thing in common. They contained food. By trial and error our parents worked out which goods would survive the postal system, and if it arrived in one piece and could be eaten, they sent it. If we didn't like the contents ourselves then someone else would be glad of them and nothing was ever wasted.

To appreciate a feast, one must first of all experience a fast. During my teaching days I frequently enjoyed being part of the school camp team and was often invited join in 'midnight feasts' – sedate little gatherings where already overfed children crunched crisps and guzzled lemonade by torchlight. I've pretended to be terrified of intruders and agreed that 'we'll all be in terrible trouble if we're found out.' I would not dream of spoiling their fun by telling them that midnight feasts were timetabled as carefully as any other event during their week, and that midnight never occurred at nine-thirty.

Without fail as I crept back to my room to wash off the chocolate before easing my exhausted body into bed my mind would turn to other feasts. Then the fear was real. The punishment for being caught out of bed after 'lights out' was bad enough, but to be caught three or four to a bed, eating, had you straight up before Mother Superior the following morning. She was small, but she was terrifying in anger and could verbally reduce you to a snivelling wreck before stopping large amounts of your precious 'out time'. We were never, never, allowed to get into another girl's bed. I had no idea why this rule was upheld so strictly. Now I know and I still think the nuns had nothing to fear but their own fears.

Food parcels, as I have already mentioned, were always received with whoops of delight and we got very crafty. The rules read: 'All Food Parcels To Be Brought To The Refectory. No Food In The Dorms As This Encourages Mice.' Well, we brought the odd tin of condensed milk to spread on the bread and marge or perhaps a currant loaf to our table, and put the nuns off the scent by saying that the parcel had contained new underwear and suchlike. The best of the goodies were squirreled away in lockers all over the dorms of your friends. You waited for a few days to let the trail go cold and then hunger got the better of caution and the midnight feast took place.

At the agreed time, well after the nuns' lights, visible from top dorm's window, had gone out, a dozen or so girls would creep out of bed, and, carrying their 'stash', made their way through quiet dorms into your cubicle.

There the strange and varied menu would be enjoyed by ten to twelve girls, huddled for warmth in the same bed. How we talked! In whispers, naturally, about the nuns, the cold, boys, food, clothes, boys, fears, ambitions, school, boys, funny stories about nuns and of course, home.

When all the food was gone and we were in danger of falling asleep in what was forbidden territory for all but one of us, it was over. Guests left as quietly as they had arrived. All wrappings, tins and jars, went into our satchels to be dumped on the way to school. We were very tidy and I never saw a mouse in the convent.

One night it all went wrong. On the floor above my dorm was a room called blue dorm. Directly above was top dorm, which had a safety rating of zero, as Baby Grace, the most hated nun ever, slept in a room a few yards down the corridor. Any midnight feasts involving food from top dorm were held in blue dorm, and as this was a very risky undertaking it didn't happen very often. On this particular night the food stockpile was very large. There were packets of jelly cubes, crisps, chocolates, packets of dates, bags of mixed fruit, cakes of all descriptions and a dumpling. Perhaps I should say the remains of a dumpling. It had survived its postal journey by being packed in a tin box; but the recipient had been eating bits of it on her way downstairs and there was a big hole in it. Nobody cared, however, as there was plenty left for all.

Happy girls lay there eating away and telling 'knock-knock' jokes when suddenly the air of suppressed festivity was shattered by a hissed 'N . . . u . . u . . nn!' from one of the other cubicles. All froze like statues for a second. Then there was a querulous, toothless, 'Praised be the Lord Jesus Christ!' from the top of the stairs. From lights out to rising bell this was the only acceptable form of communication and you answered, 'Praised for ever more, Amen!' That is if you had just been to the toilet or had gone to get a drink of water etc., and happened upon a wandering nun, not if the nun was a toothless Baby Grace and you were sitting ten to a bed eating crisps. Like silent arrows from a bow girls fled in all directions. Then there was an almighty crash and a black, squawking bundle landed on the floor. Baby Grace, trying to creep down the stairs, had trodden on a lump of dumpling and had taken half the flight in one screaming step.

None of the partying party offered first-aid, as getting back to bed undetected was first priority. One of the loyal non-participants picked the unharmed but dazed nun up and gave her a convincing explanation of nightmares and sleepwalking. Another made sure that her skirts remained over her face until order was restored. I think she was so glad to get out of it with what was left of her dignity that we heard no more about it. That was a midnight feast.

Apart from the letters from home and the gratefully received parcels the post-table gave us another bit of excitement when we discovered pen-friends. Naturally, we were all very interested in boys and most of our free time was spent talking about them. Locked up as much as we were, we could do little else about it. The school was co-ed, and sometimes innocent little romances flourished against all odds. Glen Nevis in all its glory was on our doorstep and we were 'let out' on Saturday and Sunday afternoons. A trip to the local cinema and a walk up the glen were always more exciting if you were holding hands with a boy, however pimply. That's as far as it went. Holding hands and a chaste kiss or two; but we felt very decadent.

One of the Barra girls surprised us all one day by producing a letter with a German postmark. 'Look at this,' she said 'It's from my pen-friend, Gunther.' This was really exciting. We all gathered round and practically grovelled at her feet until she showed us the letter. It was very formal and the greetings and salutations reduced us to tears of laughter. The information that 'I am two yards big' went down very well, and I am still trying to figure out what 'My father is gratitude a carved fish' was all about. Poor young German boy. He really made our day.

From then on we all had pen-friends. We wrote to boys who advertised in some magazine, and if the information they gave us about themselves was as fictitious as that which they received who knows what they were really like? Naturally we lied about age, vital statistics and looks in general. All our parents became Lairds overnight and those of us who didn't have cars had yachts. The Convent was explained away as a kind of finishing school, and we got many letters to pass around and giggle over. It got a bit complicated, the way lies do, and after a while the whole thing petered out.

Gunther, however, persevered. As his English improved his ardour increased. Letters were not enough. A very large, very soggy parcel stood on the post-table and stank the place out one day. Gunther had sent his 'Beautiful Scottish Thistle' a half-pint bottle of 4711 perfume and it had not had a good journey. The nuns were a bit cross about it all and there was some explaining to do. Come to think of it our time with the sisters made many of us into pretty convincing liars. We thought of it as self-preservation.

Having prepared his ground Gunther announced in his next letter that 'Your letters make me want to survey you . . .' That . . . 'I am coming to you expidentious' . . .

and 'You and I quite alone will roam around the countryside'. The letter caused a bit of a panic and she decided to stop writing in case he turned up at the Convent and got her expelled. The next thing that came was a telegram: 'Show signs of life! Love to you. Gunther'.

Then it all went quiet and no more was heard. After many months of silence she confessed to us that she had sent him a telegram, supposedly from her brother, informing poor German Gunther that she had died. We wondered if he would try to come to the funeral but we never heard any more about him.

Another important but extremely noisy event on the Fort William sporting calendar and beloved of the Hostel boys was the six-day motorcycle trials. Legions of motor cycles roared through the town, having raced there from Edinburgh. For the next few days bikes and riders would be pushed to the limits of their strength in endurance trials over some very rough terrain. The traditional climax was the ascent of Town Hall Brae. The bikes roared past the school and boys and masters alike would discuss the merits of their favourite riders in the world of motor cycle trials and races. I can remember the name Geoff, or was it Jeff Dukes being mentioned. We girls had no interest in the subject but the boys, including my brother and, I suspect, the masters too, ran a book and stood to gain or lose money as the winners emerged.

In the summer, at the end of the school year the local Junior Mòd was held. This event had been pioneered in the early 1900s, when a large percentage of the population were still Gaelic speakers. The numbers had somewhat dwindled by my time, so the fluent Gaelic-speaking children from the islands were usually very successful. It was an event we all enjoyed, and the

Winner's Concert on the last evening was not to be missed. One year the gold medallists from the Senior Mòd, a stunning young couple, announced their engagement during the concert and the Convent girls swooned about the romance of the occasion for years.

There was little or no Mòd coaching available to us at school, probably because the teachers were busy with the curriculum and the preparation of pupils for exams. The Gaelic speakers on the faculty were asked to judge some of the events, and this they did. A competition programme was circulated in school and you just found out what the category requirements were and entered your name against your chosen events.

Due to my accelerated race through primary school I could enter a simpler section than most of my classmates, so, feeling confident, I put my name down for a few competitions. The day before the Mòd I found out that my brother had entered me for everything else on the list. Touched by his confidence in my abilities, I spent the night before the Mòd learning poems and practising Unseen Reading and generally being a nervous wreck. Towards the end of the next day and what had been a very successful Mòd, knowing that I only had one more event to win and I'd have the Kilmallie Quaich, a large silver trophy in my grasp, I felt very grateful to Donald John. I sat in a room with the last remaining competitor in the Proverbs Knockout Competition and I was touched to see him and his friends watching from the door. They hissed at me: '*Fad's bhios slat 'sa choill bi faoil 'sa Chaimbeul,*' the ancient saying of the Clan MacDonald after Glencoe ('While there's a tree in the woods there'll be treachery in a Campbell'). As the judge was a Mr Campbell, and a very strict teacher with whom most of us had crossed swords in class, I ignored their coaching from the sidelines and came up with a proverb of my own. My opponent dried up and I had won the event and the cup for my points overall. My treacherous brother and his friends were winners too. They had won a nice bit of money from the Hostel Book on which I had featured as an outsider at 15 to 1. Apparently he had spread a rumour that I was useless. I forgave him, as always.

Life in Fort Willliam was not always laughter and midnight feasts. We had to work hard to keep up with the demands of school work, and as always little petty disputes between friends could make you miserable. However the school year was divided into three terms and each term had a wonderful thing called a holiday at the end of it. So we coped with our lives and waited for the time we could get on the Mallaig train and leave it all behind for a little while.

Chapter Twelve

AT THE END OF each term we Islanders were almost hysterical with excitement at the thought of going home again. We drooled at the thought of salt herring, lobster, scones with fresh butter and machair potatoes. We couldn't wait for the church hall dances and the bliss of not hearing a bell or seeing a wimple for a few weeks. We were a very merry band indeed as we joined the Mallaig train or took the bus to Oban. Then the sailings to the islands were not as frequent as those provided by today's car ferries and the Skye bridge, which has been such a boon to non-sailors like myself, was not even a dot on a drawing board. So we found out from which port the next boat was leaving and planned our route accordingly.

The journey, at least initially, was almost as good as the holiday, that is, until the sea took its toll. It is said that travelling hopefully is often better than arrival and many times in my life this has been proved true. For instance, some dire package holidays and rain-soaked summer breaks in tiny chalets with fractious toddlers when I've counted the days remaining with dread, come to mind. When we went home from Fort William for school holidays the buzz of anticipation in the company of our peers was great, and the holiday at the end of it always too short.

The rules of Highland hospitality were part of my family creed: 'Always repay a debt and if it's a debt of kindness, pay it twice.' Many of the mainland girls had invited me home for the odd weekend and my parents encouraged me to return the invitation. They had fretted us into leaving, to better ourselves, and missed us all sorely. So they were always happy to welcome us back and were glad to meet any of our friends who had shown us kindness. Donald John never brought any of his friends home, as he tended to keep company with the Uist boys at school, and most of his non-Uist associates were girlfriends. He would not bring them home, even if it were permitted, as they would only cramp his style with the Uist girls.

The tiny thatched croft house with no running water and too many running feet had been vacated, and a nice roomy bungalow, built next to it was now the family home. My mother had all the space for which she had craved when bringing up a family in the old house. I know the numbers went down from time to time, courtesy of the aunties, but how she managed family and croft in such circumstances I'll never know.

The house had no plumbing whatsoever for cooking, washing or sanitation, nor was there any source of power other than the peat stack. I will not linger on the sanitation aspect. It involved a covered bucket in the corner of the bedroom at night and a grassy hollow with a spade in your hand during the day. Every drop of water we used for all domestic purposes was drawn from a well, five minutes' walk from the house, and carried very carefully in buckets by whichever children were water-carriers for the day. We were always sent in pairs in case one fell in, and had to be rescued. Mercifully we never fell in, but on the way home we often fell out, and we ended up bickering on the doorstep with half-empty buckets. Back we went with swinging buckets and stinging bottoms. My mother had never read progressive books on child-rearing; she had no time. She always said that her training at Hawkhead Asylum was all she needed to help her cope with us and our father.

Even with the additional room in the new house you had to be careful with your invitation. Holidays were precious and if the girl didn't fit in, your own holiday and hers would be ruined. Happily, all the girls who came home with me were great fun and enjoyed themselves immensely. No thanks at all to the nuns who kept trying to send their own favourites off on a free junket to the islands.

They were always imploring me to take one particular girl who was spoilt, spiteful and sulky. I'm sure she had many good points, but they were well masked. She was not too bright either. When asked in Home Economics what she would do if visitors came and she only had a loaf of bread, some butter and a tomato she looked blank. 'Make a sandwich with the tomato,' said her teacher. 'Don't be daft' was the reply, 'It would roll off.' I'm afraid that her chances of ever coming home with me had been reduced to nothing the evening she told the entire Convent study group that I hadn't cleaned the bath.

The girls threw themselves into croft work with the rest of us and loved listening to my father's stories of

events on the island during my absence. He loved an audience and no question was left unanswered:
'Who did the plumbing for your new house, Mr Mac?'

'Well, now it was this man from the mainland called Jock. *Am plumair mór* (the big plumber), we called him in Gaelic. He was a nice man and a good plumber too, but he had two faults. One was foul language and the other was that he read in the lavatory. We had always managed matters of nature in our own way before the building began but knowing that some builders would be coming from the mainland we built a wee wooden house and put an Elsan, chemical toilet, in it, so that they could do their business in comfort and privacy. Jock found the wee house much to his liking and spent a lot of time in there reading magazines and books.

I didn't mind. He always came to work early and carried on as long as the light lasted and as you've seen, days are long on South Uist. He didn't believe in God so Sunday was just another working day to him. Yes, I was happy. Work was going well on the plumbing until the explosion.'

We had been drifting off a bit and wondering where the story was going, but now he had our full attention. 'Explosion?'

'Well you see, it was like this. One day Jock was sitting on the throne, deep in Mickey Spillane, when your mother called, "Tea, Jock?" Now, Jock ran on tea the way a motor car runs on petrol, so he shouted back, "Be right there, Missus!" and the very next minute there he was. There was an almighty bang and the wee house fell apart and

149

there stood Jock, clutching his trousers, book still in his hand and, if you'll pardon the expression, covered in glory. He was so taken with the yarn he had been reading that had quite forgotten where he was. When the call for tea came he just stood up and threw his fag in the the toilet. Bad mistake with a can full of chemicals. He just stood there and swore for ten minutes without repeating himself. My, but *am plumair mór* had a fine command of the English language.'

As we laughed our heads off at the picture his words had painted he added: 'So don't let me catch any of you smoking in my new bathroom.'

The one thing the mainland girls disliked intensely was the Sunday Mass at St Peter's church. Although the main part was conducted in the familiar Latin all the hymns and the long, long sermon were in Gaelic. Even after the local boys had been covertly assessed there was always an interval of boredom. 'That awful sermon would make me an atheist if I lived up here,' they'd say. One Sunday, just as the sermon was getting to the painful stage and everyone wriggled and fidgeted, there was a loud 'clunk!' from the aisle at the end of our family pew. There, wagging his stumpy tail, standing over a large stone was Sandy, our black dog. He had retriever blood in him and kept trying to prove this by presenting us with retrieved stones hours after they had been thrown for him. The sermon didn't seem half as long that day.

Now that we were older the church provided us with more than a boring Sunday sermon. It was the social centre of the community. There were concerts and whist drives and of course dances in the hall across the road.

The music was provided by some of the very accomplished accordionists on the island, and apart from the boy/girl thing and showing off your latest hairstyle, the dancing itself was sheer joy. We mainly danced the Scottish country-type dances but the quickstep was just coming into vogue and we followed the trend. My mainland friends always loved our dances and were never short of partners. Uist men are of course tall, good-looking and well-mannered, or perhaps I am biased; anyway the girls were well pleased with the selection on offer.

My parents were liberal but not stupid, and we had to come straight home after the dance. If we had a boy in tow we brought him in and gave him a cup of tea before sending him on his way with a quick goodnight kiss if he was lucky. Somehow my father was always around to check up on what he called 'camp followers'.

Drink was not sold at the dances and no one who looked drunk or carried a bottle was allowed in the hall, and this made our parents more comfortable about our moral safety. It worked, as a rule, but one night we met James who was the exception.

At first sight James, whom I had not seen before, looked attractive and a cut above the usual. He was dressed very smartly in a fine navy-blue suit and Maureen, my convent friend and I agreed that he was 'with it'. Having worked for a few weeks in Glasgow he spoke entirely in English, and although he danced with both of us I was obviously the object of his pursuit. I wasn't complaining, and after a couple of dances consented to his walking me home at the end of the evening. He didn't monopolise me and I carried on dancing with my usual partners with an odd dance with James in between.

As the evening went on I began to regret my choice. The suit still looked good but the person inside it wasn't wearing half as well. James had obviously worked out a way of 'tanking up' away from the priest's watchful eyes and was getting more and more drunk. His English was peppered with 'sort of this' and 'sort of that' and now and then he'd look me straight in the eye and say, 'I've been in love with you for weeks but I've never seen you before.' Then he'd laugh like a donkey. The first time he said it I thought he was funny, but it wore off.

Maureen had no escort that evening so we walked home after the dance in a threesome, giving James broad hints as to the desirability of his drowning himself in the canal. He was still there, however, when we arrived home, and although we said, 'Goodnight then, we'll see you,' hoping that he would take the hint, he followed us into the house. My father took one look at him and whispered to me, 'Which one of you won the tailor's dummy in the raffle?' I dragged him into the kitchen and told him the story while Maureen settled James into a comfortable chair by the open peat fire. She was enjoying my discomfort and wondering how things would turn out. She didn't have to wait long. When my father and I came back from the kitchen with cups of tea the gallant suitor was fast asleep. 'I thought so,' said my father, bending down to take a good look at James's face, 'I know him. He lives a good ten miles from here. Let him have his sleep. He has a long way to walk home and it's raining. I'll leave the front door unlocked and he can let himself out. Let's all get off to bed. You mind and lock your doors!' So we left 'Sort of . . . James', sort of . . . sleeping in the chair.

When my mother got up next morning James was still there. He was lying in the hearth, with his lovely navy-blue suit covered in fine grey ash from the now dead peat fire, sleeping like a baby. When he had been partially revived with a cup of tea he focused his bleary gaze on the mantel clock and exclaimed, 'God Almighty! My sort of . . . grandmother is being sort of . . . buried today and I am sort of . . . late!' With that he thrust the cup of tea at my mother and ran off through the fields towards the church. As he wasn't familiar with the geography of Kilpheder he very nearly ended up in the canal and had to do a quick side-track up the soggy bank to the bridge. I would have liked to have seen the look on the other mourners' faces when James eventually lined up beside them in his muddy shoes and navy/ash suit.

Ceilidhs were the high point for winter visitors, the girls who were brave enough to brave the crossing for the Christmas break. The weather was always blustery, so many evenings were spent at home. The local 'talent' as we called the young people who came to have a look at the mainland girls, would join the usual friends who came to our house. We would spend the evening telling tales, singing songs or playing 'catch the ten', a whist-type card game which I have never seen played anywhere else.

By now the piano, which had been my mother's solace when she had unwillingly returned to the island so many years ago, had given up the ghost. My father had been going to bring it in from the old house when they moved, but he found that in addition to the damage caused to it by damp over the years, the back was full of woodworm holes. So the dear old instrument, which had provided us with much pleasure and had looked so out of place on the sanded floor, was not fit to be transferred to more suitable surroundings. It became two coffee tables and the rest was dumped. In its place we had a new radiogram and a good supply of large black 78-rpm records, mostly of Gaelic songs and Scottish dance-band music. In addition, young Donald was a good accordionist, so if there were enough of us, young and old, we'd have an impromptu dance right there in our living room. Carpets were no problem. There was only lino with a few rugs which were easily rolled up.

On short winter days when the cows were snug in the byre, crofting chores were governed by the hours of daylight, so we made our own entertainment, stayed up late and slept till we woke up. A very welcome change from the regimented routine of the convent. The ceilidh would often go on till well past midnight. When things began to flag, my father, who had to be up and ready for picking up by the factory lorry in the morning, would give the signal for dispersal. He did this by launching into the longest dreariest song in his enormous repertoire, a 28-verse panegyric guaranteed to oust even the most determined hearth hugger. 'Well, well,' he'd say, 'It's a strange thing. 'Oran Mór Mhic Leoid' (Macleod's Lament) can clear the house faster than an air-raid warning. It's a pity I didn't think to offer my services in that line during the war. It would have suited me much better than the Home Guard.' As the people left he'd carry on singing, pausing only to nod in acknowledgement of farewells, and, following the last person to the door, would turn the key in the lock before delivering a final verse of his own composing, making pithy comment on events of the evening and the young hopefuls.

The shopping arrangements were another novelty. Of course they met Willie Jordan and heard his yarns and lined his pocket. He always had a soft spot for a young, pretty face and he'd put a nice hankie or even a scarf in the parcel with their purchases. The nearest shop was small, but carried a vast stock of the needle-to-an-anchor variety. As the Co-op had been extended and stock upgraded, this shop had tried to keep pace, but being a family-run enterprise they did not have the training or the space to ensure an efficient stock control system. The owner's motto was: 'No purchase too small and no hour too late.' At least it seemed like that. He once sold us a packet of 'Kirbi grips' priced at two old pence at ten o' clock at night, dressed in his pyjamas and dressing gown, having spent a good fifteen minutes searching for them by torchlight in the store adjacent to the shop. The shop itself was no larger than one of today's single garages and had no refrigeration, yet he supplied meat and other perishable goods, sometimes a bit 'high', though I can't remember a single case of food poisoning being reported.

In even earlier times most merchants had owned their own primitive slaughter-houses. When I was little I once went into one of those places with my father who was delivering a message to the shop owners, and I saw a sheep being killed. It was horrible. The large vein in the throat was cut and the sheep was just held by the horns and the feet until it bled to death. It did not struggle in any way as its blood gushed into a bucket, but I can see the poor beast's large hopeless eyes looking at me until they finally closed. I was told that it was a painless death and that the sheep merely thought that it was falling asleep, but I wondered, even at that early age, which sheep had come back to impart that information.

The merchants had a system of slaughtering on alternate weeks when the demand was low, and they shared the meat. Everything was seasonal, and if the islanders had been slaughtering their own sheep or there was a glut of herring, the demand for shop-bought meat went down. Sometimes the reverse would happen, and demand was high. At such a time, rumour has it, one shopkeeper would send the other a telegram saying, 'Send no meat. Killing myself tomorrow!' It makes perfect sense in Gaelic but assumes a more sinister sense in translation.

The girls were astonished by the size of the cod, ling and other white fish which my father brought home from Lochboisdale when the Eriskay boats came in. They had exactly the same reaction as I had to the enormous lobsters with which he delighted in terrifying them. We went cockling with iron rakes, but even when my mother minced the cockles and made them into tasty fishcakes with chopped eggs and mashed potatoes they refused to eat them, declaring that it would be like eating snails.

So the visiting convent girls had a glimpse of a life totally unlike their own, and I'm sure that none of my young friends who came to Kilpheder ever forgot the experience. Judging by the number of pleas I had for second invitations it was an interesting and enjoyable part of their education. My parents always loved the housefuls of young people who gathered around us during the holiday, and they too looked forward to the next time.

Chapter Thirteen

EVERYTHING BECOMES HUMDRUM AFTER a while, and so it happened with convent life. After two years, I was beginning to feel the constraints of having to be in at five each evening and seven o'clock at weekends. The Fort William schoolgirls who lived at home seemed to be evolving into young ladies with interesting lives outside of school. We convent girls, on the other hand, appeared to be caught in a time-warp of navy-blue uniforms and the dreaded beret. With hindsight I think it reminded me too much of the ever-present sense of being at school for twenty-four hours a day, seven days a week, which I felt during my time with the aunties. So when my age-group were given an option of moving out and boarding with local families, it seemed like a good idea to join the small exodus which took place. Donald John had finished his Fort William schooling. He had moved down South to Aldershot Barracks to do a compulsory term of National Service, prior to joining the Meropolitan Police Force. Suddenly he was grown up and out in the world, and I suppose that thought added to my discontent.

There had been changes at the school too. The previous Easter had seen the departure of a familiar and well-liked figure from the staff. 'The Boss', as we called him, Mr Charles Mitchell, who had been headmaster there since 1934, retired. He had always taken a special interest in the island children and knew most of us by name. During his summer holidays he'd tour the Hebrides and pass through Uist. He would call into our house for a few minutes, to drink a quick cup of tea and talk to my parents. I don't know if he called on the parents of all his island pupils, but I'm sure he tried. Afterward, seeing his tall, slightly stooped figure walking around the town, often with a rolled-up umbrella in his hand, was a link with home. Many people missed him when he left. I know that I did.

We needed written permission from our parents to show the nuns that they were willing to let us spread our wings, so I had a bit of persuading to do. My friend Janet and I decided to stick together and try to find a place that would take us both. It was a very exciting prospect. We had been treated like little girls for too long. This was our chance to be grown up. So we decided to try and find lodgings in the neighbouring village of Inverlochy. Janet was older than me by the best part of two years, and I was quite happy to let her do the hunting while I concentrated on selling the idea to my parents. She knew that if my parents agreed, her's would follow suit. All we could think of was that never again would we have to be in for the night at five and that the weekends would be ours. The teenagers' dances at K.K. Cameron's loomed large in our plans.

Our families agreed without too much trouble, but they insisted that we find a place with a good Catholic family, preferably one with an island connection. This was difficult. Janet's search in Inverlochy had proved fruitless. Most Catholic families were too large to have any rooms to spare, and they quite rightly considered that the best place for teenaged Catholic girls was the very place which we were so anxious to leave. Pretty soon we were prepared to lie to our parents about the religion part and take anything going, at least on a temporary basis.

We found the perfect place, with a young couple, who lived a stone's throw from the convent, in Tweedale Place. Mr and Mrs Murtagh, Margaret and Bob. They had a baby daughter to whom they always referred as Baby, and a long-haired dog called Rupert. The advert read, 'Young family offers accommodation to two girls sharing. Husband working away from home Mon.-Fri. Low rent, as company appreciated.'

We had no experience of looking behind the printed word in adverts and immediately paid our deposit and arranged to move in. A posse of Hostel boys was organised to help with our flitting and I said goodbye to the nuns and the three green curtains which had served as my bedroom walls for two years.

Both Murtaghs were there to welcome us, and Bob told us how pleased he was that his wife would have company during the week: 'She's only a wee lassie hersel' ye ken.' She was much younger than him and quite glamorous in a tarty sort of way. I kept wondering what Sister Paul Mary would have said about the eye make-up. The devil would certainly have featured strongly in her comments. However, we were only looking for the positive in our new independent frame of mind.

It soon became quite clear that life with Margaret and Bob was not going to be much fun for us. Margaret only wanted us for baby-sitting. She had her fancy man for company during the week. The lonely little wife waiting patiently for her husband only existed in poor misguided Bob's imagination.

We got to know Baby very well, and a dear little thing she was too. We walked the floors with her many an evening while we tried to get her to sleep so that we could do our homework. As soon as Bob came home at the weekends we were effectively locked out from early morning till late evening. 'Bob needs his rest, ye ken.' I think she wanted to keep us away from him in case we let anything slip about her weekday man. As for lunch or dinner, on week-days we ate school lunches and had beans-on-toast or egg-on-toast for tea. At the weekends she told us: 'Yous can make your own arrangements for meals at the weekend. Didn't I tell yez? It's not included in yer rent.' We spent many a cold, wet, hungry, penniless weekend walking up and down the streets of Fort William and sitting on a bench on Alexandra Parade, literally all dressed up with nowhere to go. We managed to go to one or two teenagers' dances, but most of the time our money went on fish suppers from the chip shop down by the station.

I became very familiar with the statue of *An Uasal Urramach Domhnall Camshron* (The Honourable Gentleman Donald Cameron), twenty-fourth Chief of the Clan Cameron of Lochiel as he gazed benevolently at us, from his plinth. We read the names of the young men who had given their all in the service of their country. Sgt K.J. Cameron of the RAF, and the names McInnes, MacDonald, MacPherson, MacPhee and even McMillan were there, all *Dileas Gu Bàs* (Faithful Until Death). They all got a little prayer from us as we sat on the bench by the War Memorial. We were particularly in tune with the war dead, as our history teacher had taken a group of us to see the controversial new Commando memorial on the Inverness road. It had recently been unveiled by The Queen Mother, and, although not everyone liked Scott Sutherland's nine foot high monument, we had found it very thought provoking.

One faint gleam in the darkness of the memories surrounding that period concerns the time when Margaret had a bad dose of stomach cramps. She dosed herself liberally with tablets that Bob had kept in the medicine cabinet. No immediate effect, so she took a second and then a third dose. Soon she was well enough to get dressed ready to meet her weekday man. 'Off tae the Braxy an' not a word to Bob, min'. Ye'r only young while ye'r young!' The Braxy was a dance hall in Inverlochy. It was hard to dislike Margaret. In a way I think we secretly admired the fact that she had two men dancing attendance on her. We noticed that her long auburn hair looked particularly glossy that evening and it turned out that the tummy tablets were actually Rupert's mange tablets, and she'd taken six.

We kept in touch with our convent friends. In fact we were free to go in and have a chat and a cup of tea with them after school any day, and this was very welcome. As you can imagine, some nuns made comments about 'Paying in St Peter's and praying in St Paul's', but Paul Mary was always very pleasant to us and encouraged the visits. Naturally we did not tell it like it really was. Loss of face was to be avoided at all costs. We regaled girls and nuns alike about life on the outside, and if we varnished the truth a little, then they were not to know.

Even letters from home didn't seem to have the same warming effect as before. I was aware that I was being economical with the truth in my replies, as I had not told them about the cold, hungry weekends. They, thinking that food parcels were no longer necessary and that our landlady would be offended if they sent any, unwittingly added to the problem. However, now and then my fathers letters still had the power to lift my spirits, even while some of his news disturbed me:

> Your mother is in hospital for a few days. I hope you don't get all worried about her as it is nothing serious. She's been feeling giddy for some time and fell over the other morning when she got out of bed. She didn't hurt herself, but we thought that she'd better see the doctor and he said that a few days in the hospital, while she found her sea legs again would be the best thing. They say that a lot of women of her age get like this and I'm sure they know the right treatment. I know of a few men round here who keep falling over, but it has nothing to do with their age and the hospital is the last place they want to be.
>
> We have cause to be grateful to the good Sacred Heart nuns, they are treating your mother like a queen and I'll have to mind my P's and Q's when she comes home. The place is very quiet without her rushing around and although Donald and the twins don't say much I think they miss her too. We've got used to her strange manic ways. One day last week I came home from the factory and she was sittting down drinking a cup of tea with Peigi Mhór (Big Peggy) who was in no hurry to leave. After a while I got annoyed and asked if they knew of any other man in Kilpheder who came home from a day's work and found two gossips and an empty table waiting for him. Peigi took the hint and went off home very smartly and I got my dinner, but your

mother gave me the cold shoulder all evening. Next day I came home and what did I find but a plate of soup and a spoon on the gate post waiting for me. All the men on the lorry thought it was very funny but I think your mother had the last laugh. Mind and write a nice letter to her and send her a brooch or something pretty with the enclosed.

My mother's illness was short-lived and I think she quite enjoyed the only stay in hospital she had ever had. All the children, twins included, had been delivered by our neighbour's wife, the local midwife, in the big double bed in the croft house.

After struggling with the Murtagh situation for the best part of a term we put out feelers for other lodgings. Winter was approaching and the weekends getting colder and colder. It was easier this time as we had more scope for searching – all our weekends in fact. We were very pleased when a friend of Janet's family who had married a Fort William man made contact with her and offered to take her in. Janet told her that she and I came as a package, so, reluctantly, she agreed to take us both.

For some reason, at various times throughout my life complete strangers have taken an instant dislike to me. They take one look and I know it has happened again. I can feel it happening and haven't the faintest idea why it should be. It happened the first time I met Mrs Hodges. I just knew that she wasn't going to be my best buddy. However, despite her obvious antipathy she didn't withdraw her offer. I was relieved, because in the circumstances I didn't have much choice. We'd already told the Murtaghs that we were leaving and their next babysitters were being interviewed.

We went off on a preliminary visit. Mrs Hodges had invited us to Sunday tea so that we could meet the rest of the family. The house was small and grimy in a fairly large tenement block, close to the railway line. John Hodges worked in some department of the railways and I think the house came with the job. The evening started well, with a blazing fire promising winter warmth and a table laden with home-baked goodies – so far so good.

Mary Ann, as Mrs Hodges asked us to call her, was charm itself, mainly to Janet, and even asked me to take my coat off. As the visit progressed, her four little girls draped themselves round me and I felt that this would be a nice place to live. Mary Ann asked for my mother's address so that she could assure her that her daughter would be in safe hands. All seemed well.

My mother showed me the letter on my next visit home. I didn't wish to disturb her by correcting a few falsehoods. 'Your daughter will be given every home comfort. I will treat her as my own. She will have the freedom of the larder and the pantry . . . etc.' A total distortion of the facts. Mary Ann was the kind of person one should not meet on a dark night without a pocket full of crucifixes and a clove of garlic or two. Not a nice lady.

From the very first day she treated me with a kind of sneering contempt and seemed unreasonably jealous of my friendship with Janet. She had a very strong personality and John and the girls scuttled around trying to keep out of her way. He was an inoffensive little man, and, come to think of it, his life must have been pretty grim. Occasionally he'd try to speak to me about the way I was being treated but broke off before he said much more than 'See her. Ach ye puir wee lassie . . .' and he'd shake his head and sigh. I simply couldn't do anything right by her. She rarely spoke to me and if I tried to join in any conversation she'd treat me to an icy glare, look at Janet, nod her head towards me and go off into peals of laughter as if at some shared joke. My clothes, hair and even my brown eyes were ridiculed. 'Tell me dear did your mother know any Chinese airmen?' followed by the usual peals of laughter.

Going back to Mary Ann's letter to my mother. I was to have the freedom of the larder and the pantry. That was a bit misleading. Nobody had the freedom of the larder except Mary Ann, and the pantry was full of old sewing machine parts and wellies. I really don't know what made that woman tick. She even seemed to hate one of her own daughters and that poor child couldn't put a foot right. She was never physically abused but had to endure ridicule and name-calling and was generally made to feel ugly and stupid. Her and me both.

Once or twice things got mislaid, as they will in any household, however tidy. Mary Ann's brooch, which she claimed to have left in the bathroom, 'where anybody could have lifted it . . .' (Glare in my direction), went missing one day. There was a great flurry of looking in corners amid bits of innuendo aimed at me. My side of the bedroom was thoroughly searched, pockets turned out in my clothes and even my mattress turned. I'd nothing to fear but felt so embarrassed. The beastliest thing of all was that she turned to Janet and said, 'Of course I know who your people are, Janet,' and she didn't search an inch of her space.

Fortunately the brooch turned up, pinned to the lapel of a jacket she'd worn the day before. There was no apology. I felt that Janet should have stuck up for me or at least not have been so firmly tucked in Mary Ann's pocket. Still I suppose she felt flattered, as our landlady paid her compliments and gradually poisoned her mind against me. Soon the cameraderie of our strange but friendly fight for survival in the Murtagh household was replaced by an icy silence.

The coldnesss between us was exceeded by the refrigeration to which we were exposed in the tiny attic boxroom which was our bedroom. It looked out on the snowy Ben and was without any form of heat, save our breath, which hung in icicles from the window sashes each morning. It's the only time in my life that I can remember wearing more clothes in bed than out of it. It shows how far apart Janet and I had drifted if you can picture us maintaining a stony silence whilst donning cardigans, socks, scarves, gloves and bobble hats on top of our pyjamas.

As I took it upon myself to meet the little girls and walk home from school with them each day, probably in a vain attempt to ingratiate myself with Mary Ann, she started to lay a place for me at the kitchen table with them. Janet shared the more substantial evening meal with her and John when he came home from work. I ate so many fish fingers in that time that it should have made me a better sailor.

The atmosphere was always very tense when I was around so I took to spending more and more time studying in the bedroom, preferring its icy loneliness to the symptoms of leprosy which Mary Ann's presence aroused in me. Soon I was told that I was using up too much electricity. So I lay on my bed in the icy darkness, listening to the trains and imagining that they were taking me to some exotic country where I would be welcomed into a huge house full of roaring fires and pleasant company, like my family. As it was dark outside I couldn't go for a walk. Anyway I'm sure that my so doing would have given rise to more ambiguous comments.

I still visited the convent, although no longer living within such an easy distance of the place. I had some good friends there and dear old Sister Paul Mary always greeted me affectionately, often expressing concern: 'You're not so bubbly, are you happy? You look smaller!' One Saturday I'd gone to the cinema with convent friends to see Bing Crosby in that lovely film *High Society*, and afterwards we sat around in the recreation room singing the songs, while a very mellow Paul Mary tried to improvise the accompaniment on the piano. The thought of going back to fish fingers and cold shoulder seemed to hit me like a physical blow. As Sister Paul Mary bid me farewell: 'Watch out for the devil and walk with God, my child!', I astonished her by throwing my arms around her and wailing like a banshee into the comforting folds of voluminous black which at that moment seemed to represent all the security in the world.

'Come now, you can't let Mother Superior see you looking like this', she led me off talking all the time, 'She'll know what to do. We can't have one of *our* girls looking so ill and worried all the time. Look at you, there's nothing left of you . . .' and other motherly mutterings. Just before we entered Mother Superior's sanctum she said, 'Not pregnant, are you? Of course not.' That made me giggle and she said, 'Humph! You're still in there somewhere!'

Mother Superior didn't have to be told anything. Over the weeks she and the other nuns had kept tabs on all the girls who had left. They had their informants. She took one look at me and said, 'Your place is ready for you. Do you want to come back?' I couldn't wait to say, 'Yes, please!' It was like coming home. A week's notice to the Hodges' ménage and I was back in and mighty glad of it.

My friendship with Janet suffered a setback, but not a terminal blow. She saw through Madame Hodges in time and went to live in other lodgings. We have met at various stages in our lives and renewed the ties of shared memories as only ex-convicts and ex-convent girls can.

My last term went by in a flurry of exams and fears about the future. Fortunately being back in a stable, albeit strict, environment meant that I had nothing else to worry about except school work, and once the exams were over we all relaxed a little. The music teacher at school produced a very successful *Pirates of Penzance* which ran for three nights at the Town Hall Theatre. As I pranced and sang around the stage as one of Major-General Stanley's daughters I remembered another music teacher who had wanted to produce Gilbert and Sullivan. It all seemed so long ago.

Even at this late stage, with only a few weeks to go at Fort William school, I fell foul of a new member of staff, a burly Highlander with a wicked temper. He was known to have a mean right hook and was what is known in the profession as a very physical teacher. One day he floored me by hitting me over the head with a thick dictionary for talking in class. As soon as I could see straight I dashed off a Gaelic poem in his honour and circulated it. The title was 'Ode to a Caveman' and it began 'Hail to thee, O hulk of meat, I know full well you think you're *it*. Perhaps it's just as well you do, 'cause no one else thinks that but you.' It loses a lot in translation and it was never Rabbie Burns's style. It was very long and had cutting references to parts of his anatomy best left unmentioned. My friends loved it and it made my head feel much better. I managed to get away with it, although some members of class wanted to pin it on the school noticeboard. I managed to change their minds for them as I already regretted my actions. At the leavers' dance I was very surprised to find my former adversary asking me to take the floor with him and being very nice. He asked about my plans for the future and holiday plans and such like pleasantries. When the music ended he wished me well and said, 'That was a very funny poem you wrote about me, but coming from a convent girl some of the language surprised me.' As my old friend, 'Mary By The Canal', would say, 'I was very put about'.

My future depended on getting the requisite number of passes for teacher-training and I had my heart set on going back to teach at one of the island schools one day. My earlier ambition, to be an art teacher, had been squashed by my father. 'Art school is full of weirdos and queers.' God only knows who told him that, as I don't think he had ever even met an art student. I knew then and know now that his assessment was totally without merit. My poor old art teacher's slip-up with the syllabus meant that I couldn't even think of going to art college anyway, despite getting a very high mark for the drawing and painting module. I was quite happy to send my application to Notre Dame College of Education, my aunt's old college in Glasgow, and hope for the best. It was a residential college run by nuns, but after three years with them I felt that I had got their measure. Some good, some not so good, just like the rest of us.

The end of this term would be like no other that I had known. I would be saying farewell to my schooldays – well, not quite. As it happened they continued until a few months ago. My teaching life followed the same pattern as my days on the other side of the desk. Beginning in the Hebrides at a little school even more isolated than Kyles Flodda, where I boarded with the very people whom John and my father had visited. They were very civilised indeed! In fact John's comment had caused them much merriment. Then I moved on to a larger school and then across the sea as I had done in childhood, but as we say in Uist, that's another story. For now all I knew was that the coming holidays would be exciting and as always enjoyable, as would all future visits to the island croft which had been my lodestone throughout my childhood.

I would see the young Queen and Prince Philip driving past our house on the newly tarred and newly named Queen's Road. (I never heard it called that again after the Royal visit.) The young Royals would visit the factory and my father would declare that 'The poor wee Queen looked half starved and her hand felt like a baby flounder.' She would look at the mountains of tangles and ask, 'Do people enjoy gathering all this seaweed, Mr MacMillan?' The Rocket Range would be disputed and fought over and eventually become the Guided Weapons Range which would bring a certain English soldier to the island. Very nice man, but with no talent for catching stirks. All this was in the future, as were my examination results.

At last the great day came and we were called into the school office. Janet, the secretary, who had been much more than a secretary, more like a mother figure to most of us, despite her own youth, sat at her desk as we went in with ashen faces. When I came out she put her arm round my shoulders and mopped my tears, saying, 'Calm down now, you have passed all your subjects, haven't you?' She had seen it all before. 'If they cry, they've passed. If they faint, they've failed.' I was upright and crying but I had failed my art exam, and although I had known in advance that it was going to happen it still hurt. However my tears were mostly tears of relief, I had indeed passed enough subjects to get into teacher-training, and despite all appearances to the contrary I was well pleased.

I joined the long queue at the post office telephone box and eventually got our neighbours to bring my mother to the phone. It was strange, hearing her voice from so far away. We didn't make phone calls lightly in those days. I told her my good news twice; she was so nervous that she couldn't hear me the first time. Her voice went all trembly as she said, 'I'm sending you a big, big postal order and you go to that Mairi Nic an t-Saoir shop that you are always looking at and buy yourself anything you want. Anything at all.' She didn't heap praise on my head, but I knew that she was pleased. I also knew that that it would take at least three of my father's weekly pay packets to buy the kind of outfit she had in mind from the shop she had mentioned, so I didn't even go in there. As I spent the money on a lovely dress in a much less prestigious shop I decided that I would not tell her where it came from. She deserved the pleasure of thinking that she had made my dream come true. At that moment I felt older and more worldy wise than my little mother and I knew that I had left the days of my childhood behind.